IPHONE 16 PRO USER GUIDE

Detailed Manual with
Comprehensive Illustration on
How to Setup & Use the iPhone
16 Pro with iOS 18 Tips and
Tricks for Beginners and
Seniors

SCOTT WHETZEL

Table of Contents

INTRODUCTION

Apple unveiled the iPhone 16 Pro on Monday, which includes larger displays, a new A18 Pro CPU, some new recording options, and longer battery life.

The screen size of the company's new flagship iPhone 16 Pro smartphone is 6.3 inches. This phone features "the thinnest borders on any Apple product," according to Apple

There are four color options ranging from natural, black, white, and a recently introduced "desert titanium." With a 16-core neural engine, the A18 Pro processor powers the iPhone 16 Pro family. Its six-core GPU, which is 20% quicker than the A17 Pro in the iPhone 15 Pro, significantly improves the device's graphics performance.

The iPhone 16 series also features a new Camera Control button. According to Apple, the button will have a two-stage shutter as part of a software update later this year. New photo styles are being introduced by Apple, and you may alter the styles in your images after you capture them.
The Photos app on the iPhone 16 Pro allows you to modify the playback speed after capturing 4K video at 120 frames per second.
.

To further its AI efforts, Apple is introducing these new phones along with certain Apple Intelligence capabilities that will go live in beta in October.

Let us walk you through your journey using the new iPhone 16 pro with this instructional manual containing expert guides and tips for beginners and seniors

CHAPTER 1

Turn On/off your iPhone 16 Pro

Turn On your device

1. Hold down the Side button for a few seconds, and then
2. Release it when the Apple logo shows on the screen to turn your iPhone 16 Pro back on.

Turn your gadget off

How to Turn Off an iPhone 16 Pro with Buttons

1. Press and hold the Side and Volume buttons on the right and left sides of your iPhone for a brief period.

Note: You should only depress the Up or Down Volume buttons. Avoid pressing both.

2. A power switch with the label "slide to power off" ought to show up at the top of the screen.
3. Move the Power symbol completely from the left to the right.Your gadget will Turn off

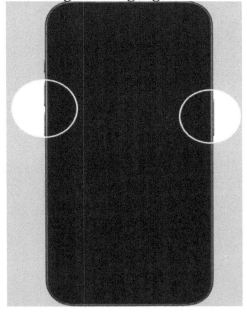

Using the Settings App to Turn Off your gadget

1. Select General from the Settings menu
2. Choose Shut Down by swiping down to the bottom of the menu
3. Press and hold the Power button from left to right.

Turn off Your device Using Siri

Telling Siri to switch off an iPhone is perhaps the quickest way to do so.

✦ My iPhone shut down when I used the phrase "Hey, Siri." Say "Shut down my iPhone" and answer "Yes" when prompted to validate the action.

Turn off your device screen

Switch off the iPhone 16 Pro's screen

If you only want to turn off the screen on your iPhone 16 Pro but want it to be able to receive calls, texts, and alerts,

1. Press the Side button once.
2. To wake it up, touch the screen or press the Side button.
3. Note: You don't need to manually turn off the screen every time you set your phone down; all iPhone models automatically dim or turn off after a few seconds. You may change the duration that your iPhone stays awake before the screen shuts off by going to **Settings > Display & Brightness > Auto-lock.**

CHAPTER 2

Standby Mode

Use the iPhone's Standby Mode

Your iPhone can show the clock, your calendar, and other helpful data when it is docked and charging.

With the addition of the iPhone Standby screen functionality in iOS 17, your iPhone may now function as an always-on display. Here, we'll go over how to set up StandBy on an iPhone, personalize the display, and handle situations when the screen won't turn on correctly.

Use the Standby Mode on your iPhone

- After locking and starting normal charging, turn your iPhone horizontally to enter StandBy mode. In a few seconds, your iPhone's screen should automatically transition to the StandBy interface.

Note: You may use a charging cable or wireless charging to use the iPhone StandBy screen.

Turn on and off the iPhone Standby Screen

The iPhone StandBy screen feature is completely deactivated and reactivated at any time.

How to turn off the StandBy screen is provided here.

1. Launch the iPhone's Settings app
2. Choose StandBy
3. Flip off the green switch that is adjacent to StandBy

Note: Just follow the previous instructions and flip the switch to activate StandBy

Modify the iOS 18 Standby Mode

From within StandBy itself, you may customize the look and feel of your iPhone's standby mode whenever you'd like. Here's how to make it appear the way you like.

1. To enter StandBy mode, turn your iPhone horizontally while it is charging. If this is your first time using StandBy, a quick welcome message will be displayed to you. Tap the x in the upper-right corner to close the notification

2. To view different StandBy displays, swipe left or right.

Note: The StandBy screens on your iPhone work in the same way as the Home displays. It is possible to customize the look of each widget and add new ones to every screen.

3. To modify the style of the widgets on the screen at hand, swipe up or down.

4. Two widgets can be supported on each iPhone StandBy screen: one on the left and one on the right. Simply long press on one side to add or delete a widget

5. Click the minus button to remove a widget from the StandBy interface

6. Click the + icon to create a new StandBy widget

7. Use the Search Widgets field at the top of the page to choose a StandBy widget, or choose one from the Suggestions menu on the left.

8. Click Add Widget to add the widget to your StandBy screen.

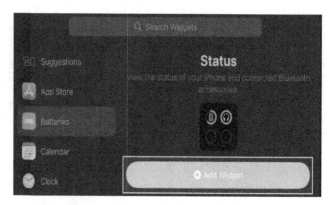

9. You're done! Just follow the previous instructions to add or delete a widget from another StandBy screen or the opposite side of the screen.

Dynamic Island

See the area at the top of your screen that resembles a pill capsule. That is the Island of Dynamic
In addition, the Dynamic Island may display real-time information about your ongoing tasks, such as connections, AirDrop, sports scores, and directions from Apple Maps, saving you from having to switch between applications
.

How to Utilize the Dynamic Island

Here are a few methods for utilizing this iPhone feature:

Modify the view

Enlarge the Island of Dynamic. Touch and hold the notice to open it in a bigger window for additional details.

1. Bring the Dynamic Island to an end. You may swipe from the right or left toward the center to reduce the size of a notification
2. Open an app. To see the app that Dynamic Island is monitoring in full-screen mode, simply tap on the application

See live activity

1. To launch the app when you receive an update, press the notification on the Dynamic Island.

Keep track of phone calls

You can keep an eye on it while on the phone. Here's how to do it:

1. To view the duration of the call, the name and number of the caller, to adjust the audio

source, or to end the call, press and hold the Dynamic Island

2. To initiate a call using the Phone app, tap the screen.

Confirm purchases made using Apple Pay.

Following an Apple Pay transaction, you may monitor the progress of your payment:

1. To verify the transaction, double-click the iPhone's side button
2. To urge you to log in with Face ID, a swirling green image will appear on the Dynamic Island
3. After the transaction is complete, a green smiling face will appear on the screen

Play audio, such as music.

You have control over how the audio is being played back. It's simple.

1. To view the audio's name and logo, enlarge the screen, pause, play, rewind, fast-forward, or adjust the audio output, press and hold the Dynamic Island button.

Create a timer.

To start a timer, open the Clock app, then:

1. To view the active timer and to pause or stop it, press and hold the Dynamic Island
2. To activate the timer in the Clock app, tap the screen

Verify the screen capture you made

The Dynamic Island shows the progress of a screen recording as soon as it begins:

1. To display the Stop button and a timer, press and hold the Dynamic Island

2. Click the Stop button once you've captured the desired content
3. You're finished when you receive a message stating that the video has been stored in your picture collection.

CHAPTER 3

Setting up the Action button on your iPhone 16 pro

The iPhone 16 Pro and iPhone 16 Pro Max now include a new Action button in place of the ringer switch. Although the Action button may be used to mute calls by default, it can do much more.

The iPhone 16 Pro Max has a specific settings menu for the Action button, which allows you to execute a variety of tasks including turning on the flashlight and opening the Voice Memo app, in addition to enabling Focus mode and launching the camera.

Apple even allows you to personalize a shortcut within select programs. For instance, you may use the Action button once again to shoot a selfie after long-pressing to access the Camera app's front camera. You may also configure hundreds of very precise actions, like messaging a specific contact, and access any program you want using the Shortcuts app.

This is a summary of the functions and configuration options for the Action button

What the iPhone 16 Pro is capable of when you press the action button.

1. **SILENT MODE**: Change the call and alert settings between ringing and silent.
2. **FOCUS**: Turn on Focus to block out distractions and turn off alerts. Choose from Do Not Disturb, Work, and Personal.
3. **CAMERA:** To rapidly capture a moment, turn on the camera. You may also select Selfie, Video, Portrait, and Portrait Selfie from the drop-down menu
4. **FLASHLIGHT:** Turn on more light as needed
5. **VOICE MEMO:** Write down ideas for songs, personal notes, and more
6. **MAGNIFIER:** Use your phone as a magnifying glass by using a magnifying app.
7. **SHORTCUT:** Use your preferred shortcut or launch an application.

8. **ACCESSIBILITY:** utilize anaccessibility feature swiftly— Classic Invert or Increase Contrast—quickly.

Setting up your iPhone 16 pro Action button

1. Launch the Settings application
   - Open the iPhone's Settings application

2. Click the Action button to select Settings from the menu.
   - Simply start typing "Action Button" into the search bar at the top of Settings to bring up the Action Button menu, and then choose it from the list of options that displays

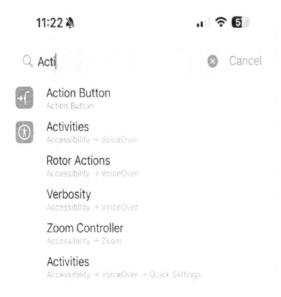

Acti   Cancel

Action Button
Action Button

Activities
Accessibility → VoiceOver

Rotor Actions
Accessibility → VoiceOver

Verbosity
Accessibility → VoiceOver

Zoom Controller
Accessibility → Zoom

Activities
Accessibility → VoiceOver → Quick Settings

3. Navigate the Action Button settings panel.
   • Silent mode is the default setting in the
     Action Options menu. Simply slide left
     to view your other options, then select
     the shortcut you wish to map to the
     Action button

4. Personalize the Action button's settings
   • You may configure specific shortcuts by selecting certain Action button options. Try to find a drop-down menu, like the one that has the Camera option. With the up and down arrows, tap the area where it reads "Photo" and choose your option, such as "Selfie."

Personalize the Action button via shortcuts

With the dedicated Shortcuts app from Apple, you can build customized Action button shortcuts for both the iPhone 16 Pro and Pro Max. This is the easiest method to set things up, however our recommendation is to build some Shortcuts within that app that you might want to utilize first.

1. Click on the Shortcuts menu.
   - To begin, swipe over to the Action buttons settings menu's Shortcuts section, then choose a Shortcut

2. Select the shortcut that you wish to use.

   • Select the shortcut you might wish to
     use from the Shortcuts menu. We'll
     launch a particular app for this example.
     However, there are plenty of choices.

3. Click on Open App

- Click the Open App button in the top right corner

4. Select the desired app

- Now, either scroll down or use a search to locate the app you want to connect to the Action button. Here, we'll go with Slack.

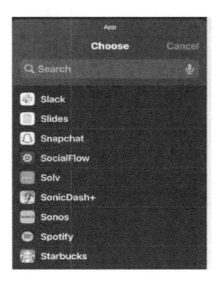

Simply close the menu now, and you may long press the Action button to open your preferred app at any moment.

CHAPTER 4

Set up and Getting Started

I will walk you through the process of configuring your device and getting started with your iPhone 16 Pro, covering everything from the most basic to the most advanced. Within this section

Setup your gadget

1. Switch on your iPhone
   - Hold down the power button on the smartphone until the Apple logo appears. Then, "Hello" will appear in many languages. To begin, adhere to the directions displayed on the screen.
   - From the Hello screen, you may activate Zoom or VoiceOver if you're blind or have low eyesight.

2. Select the phone's text and icon sizes.
   - Choose from Default, Medium, and Large for the text and icon sizes that you desire. You may preview the selected choice by swiping the icon between those sizes, which will also modify the text and graphics on this Appearance screen.
   - When you're ready, select your desired size for the icon and hit Continue.

Set up manually or select Quick Start.

On the Action button, select the Settings menu.

- Gadget for fast setting up your new one.Choose If you don't have any other devices, set up without any others.
- To configure accessibility options, touch the blue accessibility icon here.

3. Turn on your gadget network/connectivity
4. To activate and complete the device
   configuration, you must establish a connection
   with a Wi-Fi or cellular network.
   - To utilize your device's cellular network,
     press Continue without Wi-Fi if it isn't
     already enabled, or tap the Wi-Fi
     network you wish to use. You are
     required to enter your iPhone SIM card
     before configuring an iPhone (Wi-Fi +
     Cellular). You will be required to
     activate your eSIM as well.
5. Configure the device for you or your kid
   - Next, select if you want to set it up for
     your use or your kid

6. Configure Face ID and set a pass-code.
   - To enable facial recognition or your fingerprint to be used for unlocking your smartphone and making transactions, follow the on-screen instructions when configuring facial ID
   - Next, to further secure your data, create a six-digit pass-code. To utilize Touch ID, Face ID, and Apple Pay, you need a pass-code. Tap Pass-code Options to select a four-digit pass-code, a custom pass-code, or no pass-code at all.
7. Transfer or recover your apps and data..
8. To transfer or recover data from your old device to your new one, choose the method you want to employ.

- You have the option to transfer data from an Android smartphone or utilize an iCloud or PC backup.
- Select Don't Transfer Applications & Data if you don't have a backup or another device.

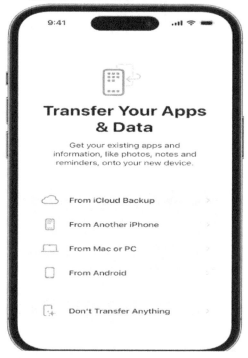

9. Use your Apple ID or another Apple device to log in. After logging in with your password, enter the phone number or email address connected to your Apple ID.
10. Optional: "Don't have an Apple ID or forgot your password?"is another option.
    - From there, you may create an Apple ID, retrieve your password, or set it up at a later time.

- To utilize multiple Apple IDs, choose Other Sign-In Options and then Use Multiple Accounts.
- You may receive a request for a verification code from your prior device when you sign in with your Apple ID.

11. Configure additional features and enable automatic updates.

To enable automatic updates to configure other features, such as cellular service, a phone number, or Apple Pay, follow the on-screen instructions:

- It will prompt you to activate or set up features and services, such as Siri. You may be required to say a few sentences on some devices for Siri to recognize your voice.

- After that, set up Screen Time by following the on-screen instructions.
- This will enable you to keep an eye on how much time you and your children spend on your devices. It may also be used to create daily app usage ti me limitations.
- After that, find out what information you may share with Apple and decide whether to give app developers access to your data.
- Lastly, to receive a sample of how your iPhone adjusts, tap Light or Dark. If you want your iPhone to automatically alternate between the two during the day, tap Auto. When prepared,

12. Choose Continue to complete.

CHAPTER 5

Apple ID

Set up & create a new Apple ID on your device

If you don't already have an Apple ID, you will be asked to establish one when you purchase a new iPhone or iPad and set it up. However, you may skip that step if you'd like, or you can use these easy steps to acquire your Apple ID if you wish to establish a new one on your iPhone or iPad.

Set up & create a new Apple ID on your device

1. Open the Settings app

2. Choose the message that says "Sign in to your iPhone."
3. The words "No Apple ID or can't remember yours" are written in blue. Tap it.
4. To get started, click the "Create Apple ID" button.
5. process of creating an Apple ID account
6. Click Continue once you've typed in your first and last names and your date of
7. Enter your email address next. You may obtain a free iCloud email address, like example@icloud.com, or input an existing one.
8. After that, enter a new password and confirm it once again
9. Select three security questions, then enter the answers
10. Select "Agree" from the menu on the bottom right when you see the Terms and Conditions page
11. Select whether you want to ignore or merge the data that is currently on your phone
12. When iOS asks you to allow the "Find my iPhone" option, we advise you to hit OK

Set up a new Apple ID on an iPhone via the App Store

First, make sure your iCloud account is logged out.

1. Open the App Store application
2. Tap the symbol of your avatar in the upper right corner of the screen
3. To establish Apple ID, click
4. Set a secure password for your new account and enter your current email address. To confirm the password, double-check it. Make

sure you input these data correctly since these will be your new Apple ID's username and password.

5. Next, select your billing address's nation. Since every Apple ID is region-locked, be careful when selecting your billing address

6. Click the Agree to Terms and Conditions option after reading the terms and conditions and privacy statement. In the top right corner of the screen, tap Next

7. Enter your name, and birthday, and select if you want to get updates from Apple

8. At this point, input your billing and credit card details. If you would want to delay setting up a payment method, select None.

9. Type in and verify your phone number, then continue

10. An email confirming your purchase will be sent to your email address by Apple. As soon as you receive this email, click the verification link

11. You may now utilize your Apple ID.

Manage your Apple ID account

Are you unsure of how to change the Apple ID on your iOS device? To update your Apple ID on your iPhone, simply follow these instructions.

Check /verify your Apple ID

It's fairly simple to find out which Apple ID an iPhone is presently logged in with. Learn how to check the Apple ID that is currently on your iPhone by following these easy steps.

1. Open the Settings application
2. Press the Name & Photo of your Apple ID at the top of the screen.

Log out of your iPhone's Apple ID

1. Open the iPhone's Settings app
2. Press the Name & Photo of your Apple ID at the top of the screen
3. After a little downward scroll, select the Sign Out link
4. You will be prompted to enter your Apple ID password if you use the same account for both the iTunes Store and iCloud. You have three choices if you utilize two distinct accounts:
   - Log Out of the Store and iCloud
   - Log Out of the Store
   - Log out of the iCloud

5. Using the toggle switches, decide which iCloud data you want to remove from the device and which data you want to keep on it
6. To delete the Apple ID from your iPhone, tap Log Out once again.

Log in using a different Apple ID

1. Open the iPhone's Settings app
2. Click the link at the top of the screen that says "Sign in to your iPhone/Sign in to your iPad." If you find a Name or Photo here, proceed as directed in Part I above
3. Type in the phone number or email address linked to the several Apple IDs you wish to use to log in
4. Type the password in.
5. You will be prompted to decide whether to merge any existing data on your device, like as contacts, calendars, bookmarks, etc., with the new Apple ID you are using to log in. If you wish to combine data, tap Merge. If not, choose Don't Merge.

Changing your iPhone's Apple ID

1. Open the iPhone's Settings app
2. After a little downward scroll, hit Passwords & Accounts
3. Select Add Account and then Mail (or Contacts, Notes, Calendar)
4. Select iCloud
5. Type your password and Apple ID email address.

6. Choose which services this Apple ID should be enabled.

CHAPTER 6

Transfer data from one iPhone to another

Transfer data to a new iPhone via Quick Start

Utilizing Quick Start, move data wirelessly to a new iPhone

1. Verify that Bluetooth is turned on and that your current device is linked to Wi-Fi. After turning it on, put your new gadget next to your existing one. To begin, adhere to the directions displayed on the screen. Restart both devices if the prompt to set up your new device vanishes from your existing one

2. Join the cellular network or Wi-Fi on your smartphone

3. Your cellular service may need to be activated

4. Configure Touch ID or Face ID

5. Decide on the data transfer method you desire.
   - Your applications and data will download in the background when you

download from iCloud, allowing you to use your new iPhone immediately away.

- You won't be able to use both devices until the transfer is finished if you transfer straight from your old smartphone

6. Hold your devices close to one another and keep them powered on until the data transfer procedure is finished. The quantity of data being sent and network conditions are two examples of variables that might affect transfer times.

Transfer data to a new iPhone via a wired connection

With a cable connection, you will be able to move your iPhone's data to a new device.

With a USB-C to Lightning Adapter and a Lightning Cable, you can transfer data over a cable connection from an iPhone 14 or older to an iPhone 16. Next:

1. Attach the USB-C to Lightning Adapter to your iPhone 16, and then attach the Lightning Cable to your iPhone 14 or prior in addition to the USB-C to Lightning Adapter.
2. Turn on each device, then follow the directions on the screen.
3. Link your iPhone 16 to the cellular network or Wi-Fi on your smartphone
4. You may be required to activate your mobile service.
5. Configure Face ID

6. You have to wait for the transfer on both devices to be completed before utilizing them. The quantity of data being sent and network conditions are two examples of variables that might affect transfer times.

Transfer data from one iPhone to another or between your old and new phones

Using a Lightning to USB cable and a Lightning to USB 3 camera adapter. Next:

1. Use the Lightning connector on the Lightning to USB 3 Camera Adapter to supply power. Use an adapter with a power output of 12W or more, please
2. Attach your existing iPhone to the Lightning to USB 3 Camera Adapter.
3. After your new iPhone is inserted, attach the other end of the Lightning to the USB Cable to the USB 3 Camera Adapter.
4. Turn both devices on, then follow the directions on the screen.
5. Link your iPhone 16 to the cellular network or Wi-Fi on your smartphone.
6. You may be required to activate your mobile service.
7. Configure Touch ID or Face ID
8. Before using either device, you must wait for the transfer to finish on both of them. The quantity of data being sent and network

conditions are two examples of variables that might affect transfer times.

Transfer data between your iPhone and Android smartphone, or vice versa

We recommend utilizing your previous iPhone Lightning cord to transfer the maximum amount of data.

You will be able to transfer lots of data or information ranging from photos, videos, contacts, calendars or events, messages, applications, music, and lots more

Make transfer via cable

Establish a link between the two gadgets.
Activate the newly acquired Android gadget. When asked, connect your new Android phone to your old iPhone via Lightning to USB-C. You may occasionally require an OTG adapter.

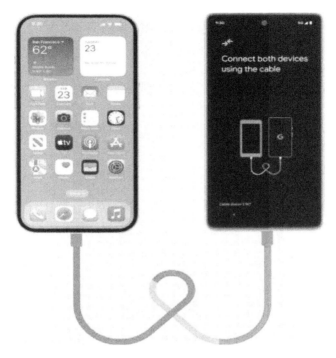

1. **Choose your information/data.**
2. To pick what to copy over, including contacts, messages, images, WhatsApp chats, and more, follow the on-screen instructions.

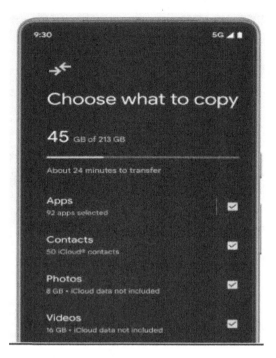

3. **Click the transfer icon**
4. And that's it. Your most crucial information has been transferred to your new or old Android or iPhone

If there's no cable available you can try out the next step via transferring wirelessly

Transfer files or data wirelessly

1. Connect the two gadgets wirelessly.

- Your new Android phone should turn on. Then, follow the on-screen instructions. Choose 'No cable' when prompted, then use the Switch to Android app to connect your iPhone and Android via Wi-Fi

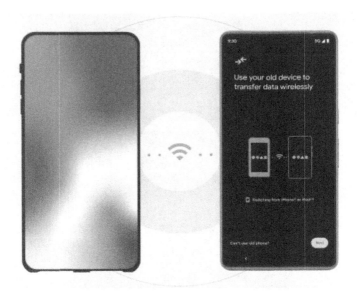

2. Choose your information or data

- Just follow the on-screen directions to choose the contacts, photos, videos, and calendar events that are included. You'll need to utilize a wire to move WhatsApp chats and messages.

3. Click the transfer icon

- And that's it. Your new Android phone now has your info on it.

CHAPTER 7

Airdrop

Utilizing your iPhone's AirDrop

Transfer data between an iPhone and a Mac or other Apple devices

Toggle AirDrop on via the control center

1. Swipe down from the top-right corner of the iPhone screen to access Control Centre.
2. To enlarge the portion that shows the icons for Bluetooth, wireless, cellular, and airplane modes, press and hold the section
3. To activate AirDrop, tap on it
4. Choose from the Receiving Off, Contacts Only, or Everyone choices on the screen that appears.

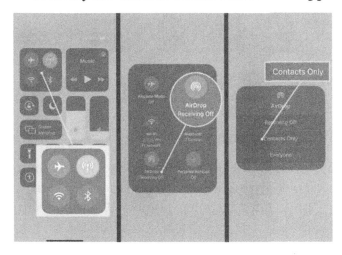

Toggle AirDrop on via the iPhone Settings

Through the Settings app on the iPhone, you can also enable AirDrop.

1. Launch the Settings application
2. Press the General button
3. Press the AirDrop button
4. Select one of the following three settings: Contacts Only, Receiving Off, or Everyone.

Utilizing AirDrop to Share Files and folders

Sending a file to a recipient:

1. Launch the app containing the shared material. To share images or videos stored on your phone, for instance, launch the Photos app

2. To open the file in a new window and share it using AirDrop, tap on it
3. Press and hold the Share symbol, which resembles a rectangle with an arrow pointing out of it
4. Tap the device or the recipient's name in the Tap to share with the AirDrop area to share the file. The icons of the closest AirDrop-capable devices that can receive files are shown.

Accepting or declining an AirDrop transfer

if you receive a file,

- The file is stored on your smartphone and opens in the relevant app if you **press Accept.**
- The transfer is cancelled and the other user is informed that you denied the request if you **select Decline.**

CHAPTER 8

Configure your iPhone's cellular service

Your iPhone needs a real SIM or an eSIM to connect to a cellular network.

Setting up an eSIM

An eSIM supplied by your carrier can be digitally stored on supported iPhone models. If your carrier offers either eSIM Carrier Activation or eSIM Quick Transfer, you may turn on your iPhone and activate your eSIM during setup.

Once the setup is complete, you can choose from the following options:

- eSIM Carrier Activation: Get in touch with your carrier to start the process of assigning a new eSIM to your iPhone. Tap the "Finish Setting Up Cellular" message. As an alternative, select Set Up Cellular or Add eSIM after selecting Settings > Cellular.
- eSIM Quick Transfer: If both devices are running iOS 16 or later, certain carriers allow you to move a phone number from your old iPhone to your new one without contacting the old carrier.

Navigate to Settings> Cellular on your newly acquired iPhone, select **Set Up Cellular** or **Add**

eSIM, and then **select Transfer** From Nearby iPhone or enter a phone number. Confirm the transfer by following the instructions on your prior iPhone.

Note: Your phone number will no longer function on your old iPhone after it has been moved to your new one.

Scan a QR code that your carrier has provided

Navigate to **Settings**> Cellular, choose **Add eSIM** or **Set Up Cellular**, and then **select Use QR Code**. (You might have to first hit Other Options.) Orient your iPhone such that the QR code displays within the frame, or manually input the information. Your carrier may require you to provide a confirmation code.

- Transfer from another smartphone: To transfer a phone number from a non-Apple iPhone, get in touch with your carrier.
- Use the app of a participating carrier to initiate service: To activate cellular service, go to the App Store, download the carrier's app, and utilize it.

Install a physical SIM card on your device

A Nano-SIM card may be transferred from your old iPhone or obtained from a carrier.

Note: iPhone 14 and later devices purchased in the United States are not compatible with physical SIM cards.

1. To eject the SIM tray, place a paper clip or SIM eject tool into the tiny opening in the tray and press inward toward the iPhone.

Note: The shape and position of the SIM tray will vary depending on the iPhone model and your country or region.

2. Take out the iPhone's tray
3. Set the SIM inside the tray. The proper alignment is shown by the angled corner.

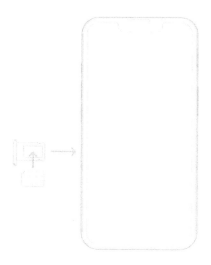

4. Reinstall the tray into the iPhone.
5. If you have previously set up a PIN on your SIM card, enter it carefully when prompted.

Convert physical sim to an esim

On an iPhone model that is compatible, you can change a physical SIM to an eSIM if your carrier allows it

1. Select **Set up** Cellular or Add eSIM under
2. Settings > Cellular, and then select the phone number using a physical SIM card.
3. Choose Convert to eSIM and follow the on-screen instructions.

Utilize dual SIM Cards on your gadget

Here are just a few of the numerous ways Dual SIM can be used:

- While making personal calls, use a different number than while conducting business.
- If you are visiting a foreign nation or area, consider adding a local data plan.
- Own distinct data and voice plans, among many other things.

Configure Dual SIM cards

1. Select Settings > Cellular, then confirm that there are two or more lines (below SIMs)'

2. Activate two lines by tapping one, then selecting Turn On this Line.

Additionally, you may modify options for SIM PIN, Calls on Other Devices, Cellular Plan labels, and Wi-Fi calling (if your carrier offers it). The label may be found in Contacts, Messages, and Phone.

3. Selecting Cellular Data and then a line, by choosing the cellular data default line.
4. One must activate Allow Cellular Data Switching to use either line, contingent upon coverage and availability.

If data roaming is enabled and you are outside of the nation or area that the carrier's network covers, you can be charged for roaming.

5. Select the voice call default line by tapping Default Voice Line and then a line.
Keep in mind the following when utilizing Dual SIM:
   • For a line to accept calls while another line is being used for a call, Wi-Fi calling has to be enabled.
   • When a line is in use, all incoming calls (including emergency service calls) that are not enabled for Wi-Fi calling go straight to voicemail (if your carrier offers this feature) and you will not be notified of missed calls.
   • When you use your Dual SIM iPhone to make a phone call from another device, such as your Mac, the call is routed to your primary voice line.
   • If you initiate an SMS or MMS discussion using one of your lines and

then wish to continue, you have to end the current chat and start a new one on the other line. and want to switch to the other.

- The line designated for cellular data is used by Instant Hotspot and Personal Hotspot.

Installing the Nano-SIM cards

Remove your SIM card tray

- Put a paper clip or SIM ejector tool into the tray's small opening and
- Press in toward your iPhone. Then,
- Note the notch on one edge of your new SIM card. Because of the notch, the new SIM card can only slot into the tray in one direction.
- Next, slide the second SIM card into the upper tray.

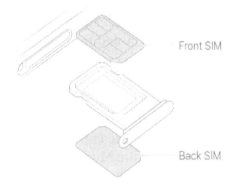

Front SIM

Back SIM

- After the two nano-SIM cards are inserted,
  fully press the SIM tray back into the device.
- The tray has a single fit and must fit in
  perfectly just as it was previously.

Knowing the Dual SIM status icons

The signal strengths of your two carriers are displayed
by the symbols in the status bar at the top of the
screen.

1. The status bar indicates that Carrier 2 is
   utilizing Wi-Fi Calling and the device is linked
   to Wi-Fi
2. As indicated On the status bar, Carrier 1 uses
   LTE, while Carrier 2 uses Carrier 1's cellular
   data.

Change the mobile device's data number

Cellular data may be used by one number at a time. Take these actions to modify which number utilizes cellular data:

1. Note the notch on one edge of your new SIM card.
2. Press the Cellular button
3. Tap the number to utilize mobile data.

Allow Cellular Data Switching permits your voice-only number to automatically switch between using voice and data while you're on a phone call. This enables you to use data and voice on the same call.

Cellular data won't function while you're on the phone if you disable Allow Cellular Data Switching and are currently on a voice call using a number that isn't your assigned cellular data number.

Take these actions to activate Allow Cellular Data Switching:

1. Note the notch on one edge of your new SIM card.
2. Select Cellular Information
3. Enable the switching of cellular data.

Manage the cellular setup

To modify your plan's cellular settings, take the following actions:

1. Note the notch on one edge of your new SIM card.
2. To modify the number, tap it.
3. After tapping each option, adjust it as usual.

CHAPTER 9

Connect your iPhone to the internet

Make use of a cellular network or accessible Wi-Fi to connect your iPhone to the internet.

Auto-Connect to WiFi on iPhone

1. First, navigate to Settings.
2. Press the WiFi icon. The network you choose ought to appear toward the top of the screen on its own; nonetheless, it won't indicate that you're connected just yet

3. Tap on your Wi-Fi network and search for the Auto-Join toggle. It is most likely not going to be green because this toggle is off.

4. To activate Auto-Join, tap it. This makes it possible for your iPhone to join this particular Wi-Fi network automatically whenever it comes into range, making it a smart option for secure networks like private home Wi-Fi networks.

Connect your iPhone to a wireless network

1. Select Settings > Wi-Fi and activate the network
2. Press any of these buttons:
    - A network: If prompted, provide the password.
    - Other: You must input the network name, security type, and password to join a hidden network.
    - The iPhone is connected to a Wi-Fi network if the Wi-Fi symbol shows up at the top of the screen. (Open Safari and browse a webpage to confirm this.)

When you go back to the same spot on your iPhone, it reconnects.

Connect to a Private Hotspot

You can utilize the cellular internet connection of an iPad (Wi-Fi + Cellular) or another iPhone that is sharing a personal hotspot

1. Go to Settings > Wi-Fi and select the name of the device sharing the hotspot.
    *   On the iPhone, if prompted for a password, enter the one displayed under Settings > Cellular > Personal Hotspot on the device that is sharing the hotspot.

Connect your iPhone to a mobile network

If a Wi-Fi network is unavailable, your iPhone will automatically connect to the cellular data network of your carrier. If your iPhone won't connect, be sure you look at these:

1. Verify that the SIM has been activated and unlocked.
2. Select Cellular under Settings
3. Check to see whether Cellular Data is enabled. If you are using Dual SIM, choose the line you wish to confirm by choosing Cellular Data. (Only one line may be selected for cellular data.)

Connect to Wi-Fi on your gadget

Join a wireless network

1. Select Settings > Wi-Fi from the Home screen
2. Switch on the WiFi. Your gadget will look for open Wi-Fi networks on its own
3. Tap the network name you wish to connect to on the screen
4. After connecting to a network, you'll notice that Wi-Fi is linked next to the network in the upper-left corner of your screen, or the upper-right corner if you're using an iPhone X or later.

Connect to a Wi-Fi Connection with an iPhone

Here's how to join a wifi network using an iPhone:

1. Tap Settings from the home screen
2. Select WiFi. The window below opens.
3. Check to make sure the Wi-Fi switch is turned on. Your iPhone can now identify and connect to WiFi networks thanks to this.
4. Press the desired wifi network to connect to. The iPhone will automatically join if the network is not password-protected
5. You will be asked to provide a password as indicated below if the wireless network you choose requires one. To connect to the

network, provide the password and choose Join.

6. If the wireless network you have chosen is secured by a captive gateway, you will be required to input a password or a combination of a username and password. These are typical on college campuses, in hotels, and at airports.

Select cellular data plans based on performance, battery life, data use, and other factors

1. To enable or disable cellular data, navigate to Settings> Cellular
2. To specify settings when Cellular Data is enabled, navigate to Settings > Cellular > Cellular Data settings and choose one of the following actions:
   o Reduce mobile data use by turning on Low Data Mode or by tapping Data Mode and selecting Low Data Mode. When the iPhone is not connected to Wi-Fi, this mode pauses background processes and automatic upgrades.
   o Turn on or off data roaming: When you're in an area that isn't serviced by your carrier's network, data roaming enables you to access the internet via a

cellular data network. You may prevent roaming fees when traveling by disabling data roaming.

Check the amount of data you're consuming

Go to **Settings>Cellular** and **choose one of the following** actions to view the amount of cellular data you have used:

- View the amount of cellular data used by each app:
  To view your list of applications, scroll down. Each app's cellular data use is displayed beneath it. You can disable cellular data use for any app you don't want it to utilize. Apps only utilize Wi-Fi for data while cellular data is off.
- See cellular data use for particular system services. Scroll down and tap System Services. Cellular data cannot be switched on or off for particular system functions.
- You may view utilization details for applications that used data while moving around, as well as data usage information for an app as of right now. To reset these statistics, navigate to Settings > Cellular, scroll to the bottom, and press Reset Statistics.
- If you have an iPhone with Dual SIM, you can view how much cellular data

you've used by entering your cellular data number.

Create a Personal Hotspot to begin sharing the cellular internet connection from iPhone

- Turn on Cellular Data by going to Settings > Cellular.
- After choosing Set Up Personal Hotspot, follow the directions in Use your iPhone to share an internet connection.

Limit how much cellular data services and applications use.

- Go to Settings >Cellular to activate or disable cellular data for any app or service that uses it, including Wi-Fi Assist or Maps
iPhone only utilizes Wi-Fi for that service when a setting is off.

CHAPTER 10

Use Safari on your device

Like Google Chrome or Microsoft Edge, Apple's Safari lets you make unique profiles for the many ways you browse. With the help of this tool, you may create distinct settings for online interactions that are personal and professional, which improves productivity and privacy.

Create & Use Safari on your device

The most recent iOS 17 release includes the ability to use Safari profiles. We'll walk you through setting up and using profiles on an iOS 17 iPhone.

Step 1: Create a new safari profile.

1. Open the iPhone's Settings app, then scroll down to the Safari app
2. Press it, then choose "New Profile" from the Profiles menu
3. You will be asked to select an icon and give the new profile a name. Once you're done, click "Done" in the top-right corner of the screen.

Step 2: Customize your safari Profile

1. Launch the newly created profile
2. Choose the extensions you want to link to this particular profile

Step 3: switching to the New Profile

1. Open Safari and use the menu button in the lower-right corner to switch between tabs
2. Click the "More" option

3. To begin utilizing the newly created profile, expand your profile and choose it.

Note: Each profile has its unique browsing history, favorites, and selected extensions.

Delete Safari Profiles

If you determine that a particular profile in Safari is no longer necessary, you can delete it by following the instructions below:

1. Activate Safari and the Settings app.
2. From the Profiles section, choose the profile you want to remove
3. Select "Delete Profile" and then press "Delete" again to confirm your selection.

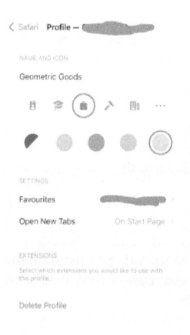

CHAPTER 11

Set up your iPhone's security

Set up Your iPhone's Face ID and Use It to Unlock Apps

Upon configuring Face ID on your iPhone, among many other features, you will be able to unlock and launch applications with just a glance at the screen. Let's begin by going over how to configure your iPhone for facial recognition.

Configure Face ID (Facial Recognition) on your iPhone

1. Launch the Settings application
2. Choose Pass-code & Face ID

3. Type in your passphrase

4. If you have already set up Face ID, you will see the option to Reset Face ID. Scroll down and
5. choose Set Up Face ID

6. To acquire a map of your face, your iPhone will ask you to place your face inside the frame and gently turn your head in a circle. After answering these questions twice, you will be connected!

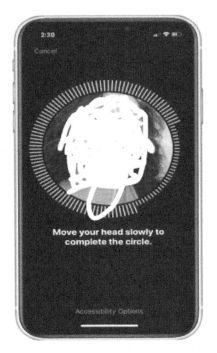

It's interesting to note that Face ID will keep learning your face over time. Therefore, don't move the phone and try again if it doesn't function at a particular angle. Enter your pass-code instead to help your phone recognize the contours and angles of your face.

Unlock Applications Using Face ID

It's time to learn how to utilize Face ID for applications now that you've set it up.

1. Open the settings for your app

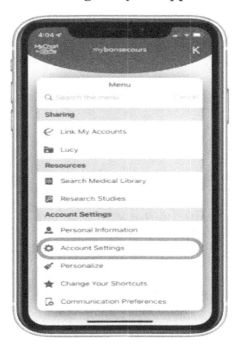

2. The process of configuring Face ID will vary depending on the app. The toggle for activating Face ID, though, is probably coming

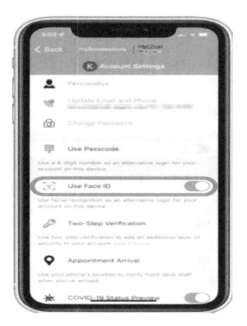

3. Go back to the Home Screen and launch the application once more
4. The app will try to unlock via Face ID.

Enable Face ID

1. Launch the Settings application
2. Choose and click an application.
3. Activate the Face ID toggle.

Using Face ID while wearing a mask

Face ID analyzes the distinct features surrounding your eyes when you activate Face ID with a mask. Face ID is compatible with all the Face ID settings you enable under Settings > Face ID & Pass-code.

NOTE: That Face ID works best when it is configured for single-face identification.

Select **Settings** >**Face ID & Pass-code**, and then do one of the following actions:

- Permit Face ID to function when you're wearing a face mask: Use a mask to turn on Face ID, then adhere to the on-screen directions

Note: When you use Face ID with a Mask, wear clear glasses—not sunglasses—to increase the accuracy of Face ID if you often wear glasses.

- Enhance your look with a pair of transparent glasses (instead of sunglasses): After selecting Add Glasses, adhere to the on-screen directions.
- Don't allow Face ID to work when wearing a face mask: Utilize a mask to disable Face ID

Deactivate Face ID temporarily

You have the option to momentarily disable Face ID for iPhone unlocking.

1. For two seconds, press and hold both the volume and side buttons
2. Press the side button to lock the iPhone right away when the sliders show.
   - When you are not using your iPhone for about a minute, the device locks automatically.
   - Face ID is activated once more the next time you unlock your iPhone with your pass-code.

Disable Face ID

1. Click on Face ID & Pass-code under Settings.
2. Execute one of the following:
   - Disable Face ID for a select few goods only: Disable one or more of the settings.
   - Disable Face ID when wearing a mask.
   - Turn off Face ID by tapping Reset Face ID.

Set your iPhone's pass-code

Establish a pass-code that must be input to unlock your iPhone when you turn it on or wake it up for increased security.

1. Select Settings, then choose from the following options according to your model:
   - Using Face ID on an iPhone: Touch Pass-code & Face ID.
   - Concerning an iPhone with a Home button: Select your Touch ID and pass-code.
2. Tap Change Pass-code or Turn Pass-code On.
   - Tap Pass-code choices to explore the password creation choices. Custom Numeric Code and Custom Alphanumeric Code are the safest choices.

Modify when the iPhone automatically locks

Select a duration by going to **Settings** >**Display & Brightness**>**Auto-Lock.**

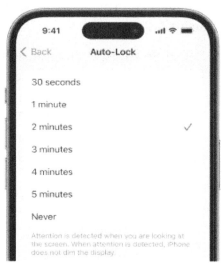

- Note: Your Auto-Lock duration is cut in half if you
  *leave your iPhone on the Home Screen without using
  it.*

Delete data following ten incorrect pass-codes

After ten unsuccessful tries at entering the pass-code, configure the iPhone to wipe all data, including media and personal settings.

1. Select Settings and take one of the following actions:

    - Using Face ID on an iPhone: Touch Pass-code & Face ID.
    - Concerning an iPhone with a Home button: Select your Touch ID and pass-code.

2. Select Erase Data by scrolling to the bottom.

Disable your passcode

1. Select one of the following after going to Settings:

    - Tap Face ID and Pass-code on an iPhone that features Face ID
    - Select "Turn Pass-code Off."

Lost your iPhone passcode

Use your Mac or PC to reset your iPhone if you can't remember the pass-code.

Stage 1: confirm that you own a computer (Mac or PC).

- A Mac or PC is needed for this operation. Make sure iTunes or the Apple Devices app are installed on the PC you're using, and that Windows 10 or later is installed. To connect your iPhone to the computer, you'll also need the cable that came with it or another suitable cable.

Stage 2: Switch off the iPhone

- If your iPhone is linked to a computer, unplug it.
- Turn off your iPhone

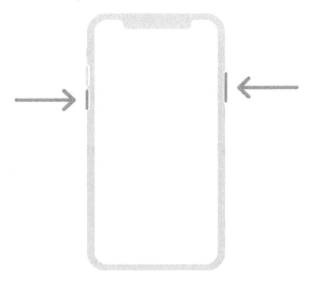

- Click & hold the side button as well as the Volume down button till the power button shows up
- To ensure that your iPhone shuts off entirely, wait a minute after dragging the slider to turn it off.

Stage 3: Launch the recovery mode on your iPhone.

1. Locate the button on your iPhone that you will need to hold to proceed: the side button

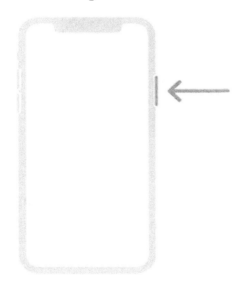

2. Immediately connect your iPhone to the computer by pressing and holding the appropriate iPhone button.
3. Hold onto the button until the Apple logo shows on it, and then release it when the picture of a computer and cable shows
   - You must restart your iPhone and turn it off if you see the pass-code screen.

- If you want assistance in getting your iPhone to display the recovery mode screen, get in touch with Apple Support

Stage 4: Use your Mac or PC to restore your iPhone.

1. If you connect to a PC, find your iPhone using the Finder, iTunes, or the Apple Devices app. (Discover how to locate your linked iPhone.)
2. When you see the choice to Update or Restore, select Restore. Your computer starts the iPhone's restoration procedure by downloading software. Allow the download to complete before turning off your iPhone and restarting if it takes longer than fifteen minutes and your device departs the recovery mode panel

3. Await the procedure's conclusion. After the procedure is complete, a setup screen will appear and your device will restart

4. After setting up and using your iPhone, unplug it from the computer.
   - If you notice a Security Lockout screen or an iPhone unavailable message
   - You may reset and delete your device without a computer by using your Apple ID and password if you've forgotten your pass-code.

Before restarting your device

- Your smartphone must run iOS 15 or later.
- A Wi-Fi or cellular network connection is required for your device
- The Apple ID and password you used to set up your device will be required.

Reset iOS 18 on your device

Note: Before attempting these procedures, get in touch with your carrier if you're using an eSIM on iOS 16 or earlier. Ask for a QR code to reset your eSIM.

1. Attempt to enter your pass-code from the Lock prompt of your device until the "[Device] Unavailable" prompt shows and your device requests that you try again later

2. Select the Forgot Pass-code option located in the lower corner of the screen as soon as you can.
3. To confirm, press Start [Device] Reset on the Security Lockout page.

4. To log out of your Apple ID on your device, enter your password
5. To erase all of your data and settings permanently, tap Erase [Device]. You have the option to either delete and remove your data from your eSIM or keep it if you use one with iOS 17 or later

6. After your smartphone restarts, set up your device once more, restore your data and settings from a backup, and create a new passcode by following the on-screen prompts

Log in using your old password temporarily if you have changed passwords recently

Note: If you utilize Pass-code Reset to change your pass-code on iOS 17 or later, your previous pass-code will remain valid for 72 hours after the change. You have to reset your pass-code again right away when you use this method to get into your iPhone.

How Pass-code Reset is used:

1. Attempt to enter your pass-code from the Lock prompt of your device until the "[Device] Unavailable" prompt shows and your device requests that you try again later
2. Select the Forgot Pass-code. option located in the lower corner of the screen as soon as you can.
3. Click on "Try Pass-code Reset"
4. To establish or create a new pass-code, enter your previous pass-code and then adhere to the on-screen directions.

CHAPTER 12

Family Sharing

Sharing Apple Books, App Store purchases, picture albums, the family calendar, and other Apple services with up to five family members is made simple with Family Sharing.

If you have kids, this is especially helpful for setting up parental controls.

Family sharing setup user guide

1. Getting started
   - First, you'll require the following two items:
   - An iPhone with an Apple ID that is logged into iCloud
   - If necessary, you may add your child to your family group after they've created an Apple ID.
   - You may edit your child's email address, date of birth, security questions, and other information by adding their Apple ID to your family group if they already have one.
   - Go to step 6 if your child is under 13 years old.

2. Family Sharing may be configured on an Apple device by an adult member of the family.
    - Navigate to [your name] in Settings. Navigate to Settings >iCloud if you're running iOS

3. Select "Set Up Family Sharing" and then "Get Started." You may invite your family members and set up your family by following the directions on the screen.

- Navigate to Settings >iCloud if you're running iOS 10.2 or below. After selecting "Get Up Family Sharing," select "Get Started."

4. Invite individuals to join your family.
    - If you both use iOS, you may add anyone with an Apple ID to your family.
    - Navigate to Settings > Family Sharing > [your name]. Navigate to Settings >iCloud> Family if you're running iOS 10.2 or earlier
    - Select "Family Member Add."
    - Fill in the name or email address of the family member and adhere to the on-screen directions. Your family member

has the option to accept or reject your invitation when they get it.

5. Invite family members
   - You may check the status of the invitation under the recipient's name after you send it
   - Select [Your Name] > Settings > Family Sharing
   - Your family members will have their names added to your account if they accept the invitation, which they can refuse

6. How to set up a child under 13's Apple ID
    - Each member of the family has to have their own Apple ID to use Family Sharing
    - It is not possible for minors under 13 to independently create an Apple ID. On the other hand, the family organizer can establish an Apple ID for the youngster in their family group and verify the parental agreement
7. Check/ Verify your mode of payment
    - Make sure you're using a supported payment method before you start. From your Apple ID account page, where you may manage and adjust your payment method from your device, you can check your payment method
    - You utilize the CVV, SMS verification code, or payment method security code as part of your confirmed parental permission to abide by regulations protecting children's online privacy
8. Create your child's Apple ID
    - You may utilize the app's settings to enable Apple parental controls
    - Navigate to Settings > Family Sharing > Add Family Member > Make a Child Account > Next under Settings > [your name]
    - Navigate to Settings >iCloud> Family if you're running iOS 17 or earlier.

- After entering your child's birthday, select "Next." Make sure the date is entered correctly

9. Click "Agree" after reading the Parent Privacy Disclosure
10. After providing the necessary details for your payment method, click "Next." You must add a payment method if one isn't already on file
11. Type in the name of your child hit "Next," and then give them an Apple ID (username@icloud.com), again hitting "Next." Select "Create."
12. To create your child's account, select security questions, and make a password, follow the on-screen directions. Select security questions and passwords that you can both recall.

- Next, enable Ask to Buy so that you may authorize any purchases your kid makes from the iTunes Store, Apple Books, and App Store. Any charges made to your account are your responsibility. Press Next.
- Go over the terms and conditions. Click "Agree."

Sharing Apple Music

Family Organizer must do the following for every member of the family to have access to the Apple Music library with a single subscription while maintaining their own private account and personal music collection:

If you're not familiar with Apple Music, either join up for a family membership or...Just switch from an individual to a family membership, and everyone in the group will have Apple Music by default.

To switch from a personal to a family Apple Music subscription:

1. Open System Preferences and choose Family Sharing
2. Open Apple Music
3. Switch to the Family subscription

How to delete family members or quit using Apple Family Sharing

It might be a good idea to discontinue Apple Family Sharing if you find yourself wanting to use the shared services and applications alone again, or if your family members are no longer benefiting from them.

Take these actions:

1. Open the Apple device's Settings app
2. On your name or Apple ID at the top of the Settings menu, tap or click
3. Press or choose "Family Sharing."
4. Next, click or press your name
5. Select or select "Stop Using Family Sharing" next.

Removing a family member from the group.

Here's how to do it:

1. Open the Apple device's Settings app
2. On your name or Apple ID at the top of the Settings menu, tap or click
3. Press or choose "Family Sharing."
4. Next, press or click the family member's name to delete them
5. Lastly, choose or tap Remove [the name of your family member] from Family.

CHAPTER 13

Using Parental control with Screen-time

1, Enable Screen Time

To control in-app purchases and impose content privacy limits, use Screen Time.

To setup Screen Time:

1. Select "Screen Time" under "Settings."

2. Select "This is My [Device]" or "This is My Child's [Device]" after tapping Continue.

- Select "Use Screen Time Pass-code" if you want to be sure the settings haven't been altered on a shared device
- Enter the pass-code again to be sure.
- If the smartphone is a child's, you may enter a pass-code by following the instructions until you reach the Parent Pass-code screen. Reenter to be sure.

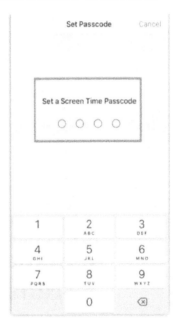

2. Restrict content

Step 1: Press Content & Privacy Restrictions in Step 1. You may enable Content & Privacy after providing your pass-code when prompted.

Step 2: After configuring your code, you may control in-app purchases, and app access, and automatically filter website content to restrict access to adult content in applications and Safari on your device.

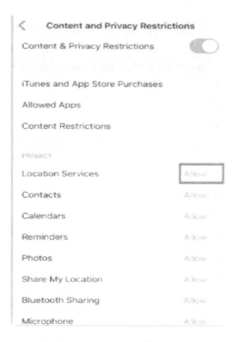

3, Manage in-app transactions

1. Select "App Store & iTunes Purchases." Select a configuration and set it to "Don't Allow."
2. Please be aware that you can modify your password settings for any other purchases you make from the Book Store or iTunes & App Store. Proceed with steps 1-3 and choose Always Require or Don't Require.

4. Guided Entry

When using an app on your iPhone or iPad, you may lock it using Guided Access. Since they won't be able to exit that specific app and it will prevent them from accessing other applications or settings, this could be helpful for kids.

To toggle on Guided Access:

Step 1: Open your "Settings," choose "Accessibility," then "Guided Access" by scrolling down.

Step 2: Toggle the Guided Access option until it becomes green.

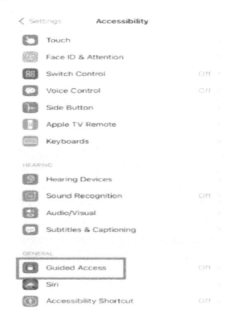

Step 3: Press the side (power) button three times to begin the guided access. The touchscreen and buttons will not function when activated.

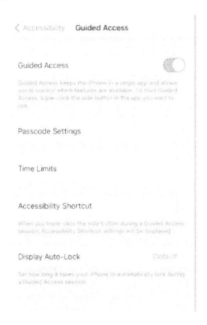

- You may also enable auto-lock features, set a time restriction, and establish a pass-code in this area.
- Press and hold the side button three times to turn it off.

Step 4: You may adjust the choices that show up at the bottom left of your screen to customize the app's settings for yourself or your kid.

- As an alternative, you may just ask Siri to activate Guided Access, and she will do it on your behalf.

5, Prevent web content

To restrict access to adult content in Safari and applications on your device, iOS can automatically filter website content. Additionally, you may restrict access to only permitted websites or add certain websites to an approved or prohibited list. Take these actions:

Step 1: Select Screen time under Settings. Enter your Screen Time pass-code by tapping "Content & Privacy Restrictions."

Step 2: Select "Web Content" after selecting "Content Restrictions."

- Select Allowed Websites Only, Limit Adult Websites, or Unrestricted Access.

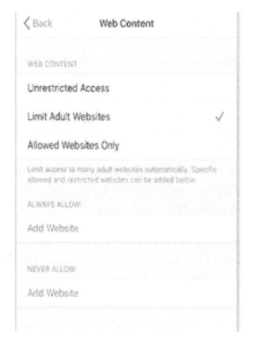

6, Restrict Siri's online search

Step 1: Select Screen time under Settings. Click or tap "Privacy & Content Restrictions."

Step 2: Enter your Screen Time pass-code if prompted. Next, choose "Content Restrictions." Select your settings after finding Siri by scrolling down.

You can limit the following Siri features:

- Content for Web Search: Stop Siri from doing web searches when you ask questions
- Block Siri from presenting explicit words by turning off explicit language.

7. Restricting gaming center

Step 1: Select Screen time under Settings. Click or tap "Privacy & Content Restrictions."

Step 2: Enter the pass-code for Screen Time. Next, choose "Content Restrictions." After selecting your preferences, go down to the Game Centre.

Certain Game Centre functionality might be restricted:

- Multiplayer Games: Make it impossible to engage in multiplayer gaming.
- Adding Friends: Prevent Game Centre users from adding friends.
- Stop screen recording so that neither the screen nor the sound may be recorded.

8. Disable tracking

You may choose whether you want applications to follow your behavior for advertising purposes if you have the iOS 14.5 update or above and use the App Tracking Transparency feature. Given that it could promote in-app purchases, this might not be appropriate for young users.

To turn off:

- Navigate to "Privacy" under Settings. Select "Tracking." When the toggle button is grey, the functionality is not active. Green indicates that something is enabled.

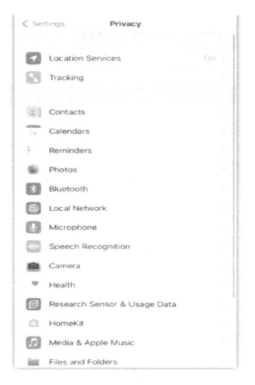

NOTE: When you run updated applications, prompts asking for permission to track your activities will start to appear if you enable apps to ask to track you. Applications will not be able to track your behavior if you don't enable them to ask for permission.

9. Permit changes to privacy settings

You may choose which applications have access to data saved on your smartphone or its hardware functions by adjusting the privacy settings.

- Navigate to Screen Time under Settings. If prompted, choose "Content & Privacy Restrictions" and provide your Screen Time pass-code. After selecting "Privacy," select the options you wish to limit.

10. Permit changes to additional features and settings

Similar to how you may enable changes to privacy settings, you can also allow changes to other features and settings.

- Navigate to Screen Time under Settings. If prompted, choose "Content & Privacy Restrictions" and provide your Screen Time pass-code. Always Allowed: Choose Allow or Don't Allow after selecting the features or settings you wish to permit modifications to.

CHAPTER 14

Facetime

Activate FaceTime

Before initiating FaceTime on your iPhone

1. confirm that your device is online.
2. Next, navigate to Settings >FaceTime and
3. Turn on the FaceTime feature.

As an alternative,

1. Open the FaceTime app and
2. Select Continue.

3. Additionally, confirm that the right FaceTime contact information is chosen.

Log in & log out FaceTime

1. Tap Settings ->FaceTime on your iPhone.
2. Select Sign Out by tapping your Apple ID under the Caller ID area
3. After a few while, select "Use your Apple ID for FaceTime" and re-enter your login information.

Make Use of the Proper FaceTime settings

1. Select FaceTime under Settings
2. Verify that the phone number and email address you gave under the "You can be Reached by FaceTime At" section are accurate

3. Tap on a number or email address and select the Remove option to get rid of it from FaceTime.

4. Next, see if your phone number or email address, from which you wish to make FaceTime calls, has a checkmark next to it in the Caller ID area.

Turn Facetime off & restart

1. Disable FaceTime by going to Settings ->FaceTime.
2. Next, give your iPhone a restart
3. Next, go to Settings ->FaceTime and enable the toggle once more.

Turn off content restriction

Simply skip this step if Screen Time is not enabled.

1. Navigate to Settings -> Screen Time on your iPhone
2. Select Allowed Apps under Content & Privacy Restrictions

3. Make sure that FaceTime, SharePlay, and Camera are enabled, then enter the Screen Time pass-code.

Reinstalling FaceTime

Reinstalling and erasing the FaceTime software is recommended if FaceTime on your iPhone is unresponsive or always displays a blank screen.

1. Press and hold the FaceTime app icon from the Home Screen of your iPhone.
2. Select Remove App from the fast action menu.
3. Select "Delete App." Select Delete one again to be sure you're done
4. Restart your smartphone now, then go to the App Store and download FaceTime.

Use iPhone Group FaceTime

Make Group FaceTime Calls

Using this procedure, you will be able to start a group FaceTime call.

Launch a FaceTime group chat

1. To start a FaceTime call, first open the FaceTime app and then hit the "+" icon. To add contacts, touch the "+" button in the "To:" field
2. Tap on the name of the contact to choose them for a call. To create a group FaceTime call, touch the + icon once more to add a contact. Until you have added every participant or have reached the 32-caller limit, you can continue this process.

To place a call after adding every contact, simply hit the video button.

Start a Facetime call & invite members to join

1. Begin the FaceTime call as you would ordinarily. Press the menu with three dots. To add extra callers to your call, touch the "Add Person" button here. Choose the individual you wish to include in the call now.

1. Tap on the group chat whose members you want to make a group FaceTime call to and then tap on the "members" area highlighted in the photo below.
2. All you have to do now is press the FaceTime video icon to start a group FaceTime call.

Enable FaceTime Photos on an iPhone

To activate FaceTime Photos on an iPhone or iPad, follow these steps:

1. Launch the Settings application
2. After swiping down, select FaceTime
3. Verify that the FaceTime Live Photos toggle is activated

By doing this, you also permit people to take live pictures of you.

Snap live Pictures While on FaceTime Calls

1. Initially, the other individual had to have activated the FaceTime Photos function.
2. Fortunately, both you and the other person will be notified when a photo is taken during the video conference. This is the second feature
3. Thirdly, not all nations and areas have access to this capability.

- After you become familiar with these, taking pictures during FaceTime chats will be a breeze.
- All you have to do to capture Live Photos during one-on-one FaceTime sessions is tap the Shutter button, which resembles two white circles nested within each other. When you tap the screen of your iPhone while on a call, this button will show up.
- On your iPhone, choose the person's tile, then press the Fullscreen button to reveal the Shutter button to take a picture during a Group FaceTime group conversation.

Add Someone on FaceTime Call

1. While on a live Facetime call, tap the screen
2. Select "Add people."
3. Enter the person's name that you wish to add.
4. Choose the individual you wish to include.
5. Press "Add People."

Using the FaceTime app

1. Launch FaceTime.
2. If the individual is one of your contacts, tap the green New FaceTime button and enter their name, contact information, and email address. Additionally, you may hit the plus sign(+) to view and select from your list of contacts.
3. To place a call after choosing your contact, touch the green FaceTime icon.

Utilize the Phone application

1. Launch the Phone application
2. To make a call, hit Contacts, then scroll down and tap the desired contact's name. Additionally, you may use the search bar to input their name.
3. To place a call, touch the FaceTime button once the contact shows up on your screen.

FaceTime with an Android user

1. Launch FaceTime
2. On the top-left corner of the screen, select Create Link
3. Choose a sharing option for the link.

Use FaceTime on an iPhone to share a screen

Here's how to share your screen over FaceTime on an iPhone running iOS 15.1 or later:

1. Launch a FaceTime call
2. To access the Share icon (a rectangle with a person in front of it), first tap the screen to display the control bar
3. Press on the "Share My Screen" icon
4. The Share My Screen icon will count down for three seconds until a little picture of your screen appears on the other user's device. When you screen share on an iPhone, your camera switches off
5. To share your home screen, swipe up or hit the Home button
6. Select the webpage, document, or app that you want to share. The other caller will be able to view your screen.
7. Those with you on the call can tap the image to view what you've shared and magnify it
8. Press the Share icon once again to end the screen-sharing session.

Take control of FaceTime's screen sharing

Here's what to do if someone on the FaceTime call wants to take control of screen sharing:

1. To view the control bar on an iPhone, tap the screen. To access FaceTime on an iPad, touch to reveal the menu bar and then hit the green symbol.
2. Press the SharePlay icon, which is a figure with two arcs in front of it

3. Press the Share My Screen button
4. To replace the existing one, tap the pop-up window.
5. Until they choose an application from the home page or a picture to share, others will see a dark screen with the initials of the person assuming control.

CHAPTER 15

Focus mode

How does the Focus Mode operate?

Users of Focus Mode can create distinct profiles according to their work, play, and leisure activities. It is possible to set each profile to silence alerts from some contacts or applications while permitting notifications from others.

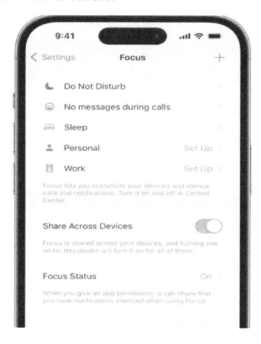

Which of the iPhone's Focus Modes are available?

To accommodate the majority of cases, iOS 17 provides a variety of pre-defined Focus Modes, such as:

- Personal: This option is great for privacy and may let you get alerts from loved ones and close friends
- Work: Designed for formal environments, this mode lets you accept messages relevant to your job
- Sleep: This setting reduces the majority of alerts to promote undisturbed sleep
- Distraction-free driving: This feature is enabled while the user is operating a motor vehicle
- Gaming: A setting intended for completely engrossing gameplay.
- In addition to this, customers can design personalized Focus Modes based on their requirements.

An in-depth look at the functionality of Focus Mode

Setup Profiles Based on Activities

1. On your iPhone, open Settings
2. Select "Focus" by swiping downward

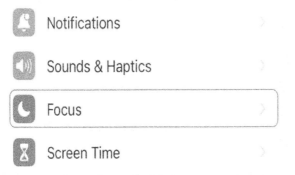

3. To establish a new Focus Mode, tap the Add button icon

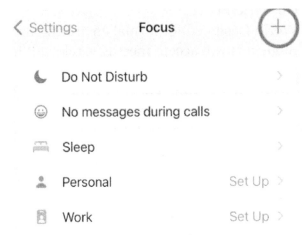

4. Select a Mode or hit 'Custom' to set up a personalized focus mode
5. Tap 'Next' after naming your focus mode (such as Work, Personal, or Gym), selecting a color, and creating an icon to symbolize your focus

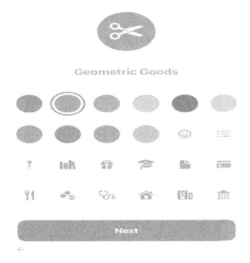

6. Select the "Customize Focus" button and configure your own Focus's setting.

Customize iPhone Notification Filters for Focus Mode

1. Select "People" from the Focus Mode menu
2. Select which contacts to "Silence Notifications From" or "Allow Notifications From."

🔕 Silence Notifications From

🛡 **Allow Notifications From**   ✓

When Geometric Goods Focus is on, notifications
from people you select will be allowed. All others will
be silenced and sent to Notification Centre.

3. Choose the "Allow Calls From" list. There are four options available: Contacts Only, Allowed People Only (whom you added in the previous stage), Favorites, and Everyone.
4. Moreover, you may decide whether to accept or reject repeated calls.
5. All calls that are routed to the Notification Centre and are not on the designated list will be paused
6. Select "Apps" from the Focus Mode menu
7. Select which apps to "Silence Notifications From" or "Allow Notifications From."
    • It should be noted that you have the option to allow applications that are not on your list of approved apps to give you Time-Sensitive alerts. If permitted, they can circumvent system safeguards like Focus and notification summaries.
8. Tap "Options" under the Focus Mode you have selected.

After that, you have the following options:

- Show muted alerts on the lock screen or send them to the notification center: Press and hold the "Show On Lock Screen" button
- Hide notification badges from applications on the Home Screen: Turn on the "Hide Notification Badges" feature
- Select whether you want to "Always" or only "While Locked" for notification silence. When utilizing this Focus, dim the lock screen. Turn on the "Dim Lock Screen"

Customizing the iPhone's Lock Screen and Home Screen in Focus Mode

- To personalize your Lock Screen or Home Screen, touch "Choose" beside the selected Focus Mode.
- Here, you may customize the widgets and applications you wish to be shown on your Lock Screen and Home Screen, or you can create a new one from scratch.

Focus Status settings in message

1. Select "Focus Status" from the Focus Mode
   options.

2. Turn on "Focus Status" so that others can
   notice when you're unavailable.

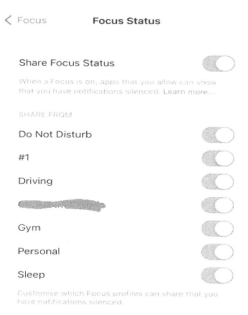

When you activate this function, everyone who contacts you will know right away that you are in Focus Mode and may not react right away. If the issue is urgent, significant, or an emergency, they can then choose to tell you right away.

Enable iPhone Auto-Reply in Focus Mode

"Auto-Reply": When "Driving Focus" is turned on, notifications from Favorites and people you permit will automatically react. In any case, they can let you know by following up with an "urgent" message.

1. Select "Driving Focus" after going to Settings > Focus
2. Select Auto-Reply

3. Choose a choice, such as All Contacts, Recents, Favorites, or No One

4. You may now personalize the auto-reply message that people will see when they message you when Driving Focus is turned on.

Setting iPhone Focus Filters

During the Focus configuration process, you may apply app filters that control what applications appear when the Focus is in use. For instance, you may set it up to display only your work calendar while your Work Focus is on.

1. Go to Settings > Focus first
2. Decide which Focus you wish to apply filters to
3. Select Add Filter after swiping down to Focus Filters.

- Choose an application, then pick the data you want to see from that application when the Focus is on.

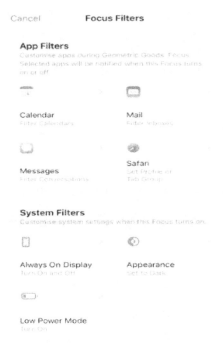

- System filters may also be used to turn on features like Always On Display, Low Power Mode, and Dark Mode while a Focus is engaged.

Schedule & switch Focus Modes with Ease

How to Schedule Your Time in Focus Mode

1. Select the Focus Mode by tapping on "Smart Activation" and turning it on
2. Go back to the prior screen and select 'Add Schedule' to create the schedule you want according to events, time, or place
3. Go back to the prior screen and select 'Add Schedule' to create the schedule you want according to events, time, or place.

Enable iPhone Focus Modes

1. To reach the Control Centre, swipe down from the upper right corner
2. Press the Focus Mode symbol. Make careful you tap on the text in the vicinity of the Focus Mode symbol. You may switch on or off Focus Mode by tapping on the symbol
3. To turn on the preferred Focus Mode, select it.

Remove an iPhone Focus Mode

1. Select Focus under Settings
2. Choose the Focus Mode that you want to remove
3. Scroll to the bottom and select "Delete Focus."

Disable or uninstall Focus Mode

Via Settings:

1. Select Focus under Settings
2. Decide which Focus Mode is in use
3. Turn off Focus Mode if it's on

Via the Control Centre:

1. To access the Control Centre, swipe down from the upper-right corner
2. To switch off the active Focus Mode, tap on it.

CHAPTER 16

Widget

You may quickly access your preferred apps and crucial information with widgets, eliminating the need to touch and slide between displays to get what you need. Front and center are headlines, weather reports, calendar events, stock market updates, battery levels, and more.

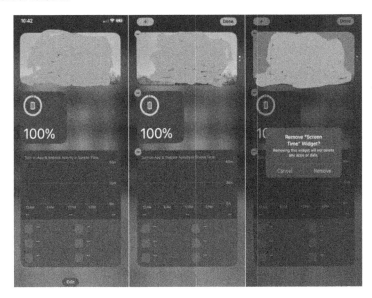

Editing and Adding Widgets

On your iPhone

1. Swipe to the right until you reach the widgets screen, which features separate widgets for the calendar, weather, news, and other apps.
2. Tap the Edit button after swiping the screen down.

3. Examine your current widgets and choose the ones you wish to remove by tapping the - symbol.
4. Once the deletion is complete, confirm it by tapping Done.

Add widget

1. After tapping the Edit button once again,
2. Press the Plus button located at the top of the screen.
3. Choose a widget to add by swiping down the list of available ones and tapping on it. Additionally, you may make widgets out of Apple's built-in applications.
4. To view the alphabetically arranged list of apps, swipe down the screen.
5. To add a widget for a specific app, tap it.
   - Numerous widgets come in a variety of sizes and layout options. To add such a widget, swipe through the layout options until you select the desired one, then click Add Widget.
   - Widgets may be added and removed, and their locations can be adjusted on the Widgets panel. Drag and drop each widget from the Edit window to a new position until they are all in the order you want. Press Done once you're done.
   - If you slide down from the top of the screen after selecting Edit, you may turn third-party applications into widgets by selecting Customize. Next, you may add widgets to the bottom of the widgets

screen by tapping the Add button next to any widget. The Add Widgets screen lists newly installed widgets at the top; press the - symbol to delete any that you no longer desire.

- A widget's order may also be adjusted by sliding it up or down in the list by holding down the hamburger symbol next to it. This groups all of the widgets you add into a single window

- You may adjust your widgets even further by tapping one to bring up a menu. To remove a widget, tap Remove Widget; to change its order, select Edit Home Screen. In certain instances, you can modify the data that the widget provides by selecting the Edit Widget option. You may choose to view messages from all of your accounts or only from a particular account and folder, for instance, using the Mail widget.

- You may press the widget to launch the associated app when it has been generated. The widget should direct you to any material it shows. To view an item in the app, touch on it if the widget has a wide layout with several items.

Creating & editing Widgets for Smart Stacks

1. You may make something called a Smart Stack widget, which shows you material from many applications and services as it changes dynamically throughout the day. Additionally, you may cycle between the material by swiping up or down on the widget.

2. On the widget screen, touch the Edit button and then the Add button to construct your smart stack. From the selection, choose the Smart Stack widget. Next, select the desired layout and click Add Widget. To view each piece of material, slide up or down on the Smart Stack widget on the Widgets screen.

3. You can layer widgets on top of each other to create your custom smart stack. When you tap on a certain widget, the Edit Home Screen option will appear. After you've done dragging one widget on top of another, press Done. Using your new stack of widgets, swipe up or down to go through all of the content.

4. Any widget stack may be pressed down to see the Edit Stack menu. Tap the - icon of a widget to remove it from the stack. To remove a widget from a stack, you may also drag it out. To adjust the order of the widgets in the stack, press and hold the widget you want to move up or down in the list. Press down on the stack and select delete Stack to fully delete the stack along with all of its widgets.

5. The Smart Rotate feature automatically moves some widgets to the top of the stack when they

have information that is timely or pertinent to show. You may disable this by tapping the Smart Rotate symbol if you'd like. When you select the Widget Suggestions option, widgets that aren't currently in your stack are immediately suggested. You may turn this off by tapping the Widget Suggestions icon. Press Done once you're done.

Add a widget to the Home Screen

1. Widgets may be added straight to your device's home screen. To relocate a widget, press and hold it, then choose Edit Home Screen. Drag the widget to the right by applying pressure on it. After that, you may add it to an empty home screen or arrange it next to the icons of your installed apps on a populated home screen. Press Done once you're done.
   - Additionally, you may tap the plus symbol in the top-left corner of the screen by pressing down on any vacant space. To add a widget, swipe down the list and tap the desired one. Select the layout and size that you want
   - Place the widget on the screen after tapping the Add Widget button. Press Done once you're done. Next, you'll notice that your home screen now contains the new widget

How to Utilize Interactive Widgets on your iPhone

Set an Interactive widget for the Home Screen

1. Switch to Edit Mode:
   - To enter edit mode, tap and hold any empty area on your home screen until the widgets and icons begin to jitter.
2. Go to the Menu of Widgets:
   - Press and hold the '+' button situated in the top-left corner of the display. The widgets menu will then open, allowing you to choose from a variety of widgets.
3. Select a Widget:
   - Choose the widget that you want to add. To enjoy interaction, for example, you may select Apple's Reminders, Music, or Podcasts widgets. Notably, only a small number of apps—mostly system apps like Phone, Music, and Reminders—support interactive widgets at this time; however, as more apps are upgraded for iOS 17, more are anticipated to have this functionality.
4. Pick a Widget Size:
   - You can pick your preferred size once you've chosen a widget. There are three sizes of widgets: tiny, medium, and giant.
5. Include a Widget

- After determining the size, you can either touch 'Add Widget' at the bottom of the screen or drag the widget onto the Home Screen
6. Complete Placement:
   - You may relocate the new widget to any desired spot on the home screen because the app icons and widgets will still bounce. Press 'Done' after you're satisfied with where the widget is located.

Configuring Interactive Lock Screen Widgets

1. To access edit mode and see the "Customize" button, touch and hold the locked screen
2. Either choose Lock Screen or make a new one
3. Simply press the button to change the wallpaper on your existing Lock Screen
4. To alter the Lock Screen that already exists, tap the "Customize" button. Next, select "Lock Screen"
5. You can make further changes on the screen that appears after this. Change the background color styles first. Select from Color Wash, Black & White, Duotone, and Natural (the default) by swiping.
   - Type the color swatch in the lower right corner of the screen to alter the style color; 12 choices are available
6. To choose a different top widget, click the date that is visible at the top of your screen

7. To modify the typeface and color of the clock, tap on it.
8. To add widgets to your lock screen, select "Add widgets". A maximum of four widgets, each in a variety of sizes, are available for addition
9. To add widgets to the Lock Screen, either tap or drag them in. You may press the Remove button to relocate a widget to create a way for the one you want to install if there isn't enough space for a new one
10. Press the close button and then select Done when you're done
11. Connect Focus Mode to Lock Screen. After tapping the Focus mode's name, pick your favorite.
12. To choose your preferred choice and end edit mode, tap the Lock Screen.

Delete an existing Lock Screen

Use these instructions to remove a Lock Screen/Home screen pairing:

1. To access the iPhone's Lock Screen/Wallpaper choices, hard press the lock screen
2. Use the left and right scroll buttons to find the combination you want to delete
3. To remove a wallpaper, swipe your finger upward over it
4. Tap the trash can symbol to confirm the deletion
5. To complete the procedure, choose "Delete This Wallpaper."

You may create and utilize interactive widgets on your iPhone running iOS 17 by following these easy instructions.

CHAPTER 17

Find My

Activate and Turn your Find My iPhone

Method 1: Making use of an iPhone

1. Launch the iPhone Settings App Icon app from Settings.

- Make sure you upgrade to the most recent version of your device

2. Press and hold your Apple ID. The Settings page will include this at the very top. Verify that the Apple ID you are logged into is the right one. You may use this method to find the position of your device on other devices

3. Select "Find My." This is located under Media & Purchases.

4. Select "Find My iPhone."

- Turn on the Share My Location button to let authorized family members and friends know where you are

5. Turn on the "Find My iPhone" icon. It will become green on the switch. Find My will be made available

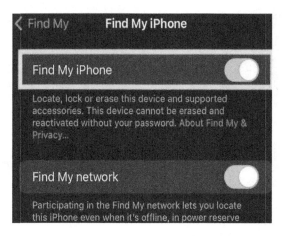

Find My   **Find My iPhone**

Find My iPhone

Locate, lock or erase this device and supported accessories. This device cannot be erased and reactivated without your password. About Find My & Privacy...

Find My network

Participating in the Find My network lets you locate this iPhone even when it's offline, in power reserve

- Turn on Find My Network if you want to be able to find your iPhone while it's not connected
- Turn on Send Last Location if you would like to communicate the location of your iPhone while the battery is running low.

6. Switch Location Services on. To locate your misplaced iPad or iPhone on a map, you must activate this function. Take the following action if this feature isn't already enabled:
   - Go to Settings
   - Select Security & Privacy
   - Select Location Services by tapping
   - In Location Services, toggle
   - Slide down and select "Find My."
   - Choose Ask While Using the App, When I Share, or Next Time.
   - Turn on the Specific Place.

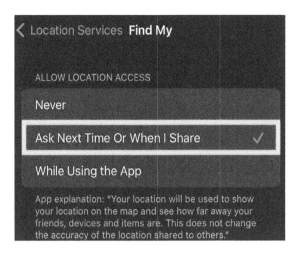

Method 2: find the location

1. Open a web browser and navigate to
   https://www.icloud.com/. From a computer or
   mobile device, you may locate misplaced or
   pilfered gadgets
2. Log into Apple ID. To log in, enter your Apple
   ID and password. Verify that the Apple ID
   you're using is the same one that you use for
   your Mac, iPad, or iPhone.

3. Select "Find My." This may be found towards the bottom of the app folder. It may also be accessed by selecting it from the App menu in the upper-right corner

4. Choose your gadget. Under All Gadgets, you'll find a list of all of your gadgets. It can take a while for the locations to update
5. Check the location of your smartphone. The position of your device should be displayed on the map. You'll see the current location if it's turned on and operational right now. You will see the device's last indicated position if it is not connected.

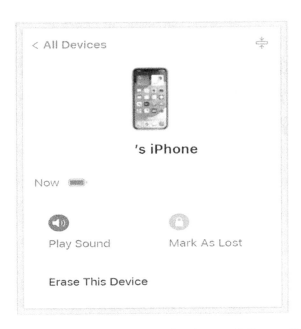

's iPhone

Now

Play Sound

Mark As Lost

Erase This Device

- To protect your device and data, click Mark As Lost. By doing this, you may password- or pass-code-lock your smartphone. To perhaps assist the finder in returning the smartphone to you, you can also leave a note on the lock screen.
- If the gadget is misplaced somewhere close, click Play Sound. This will emit a sound to assist you in finding it.
- To remotely reset your device, click Erase This Device. Your device will be completely erased as a result. If protecting your information doesn't need it, don't do this.

Locate your lost/ misplaced iPhone When It's Dead or Offline

Using iCloud or Find My

1. On an Apple device, launch the Find My app.
   - Alternatively, Use a web browser to go to https://www.icloud.com/find/ if you don't have access to an Apple device. Use the same Apple ID that you used to configure your misplaced iPhone to log in.

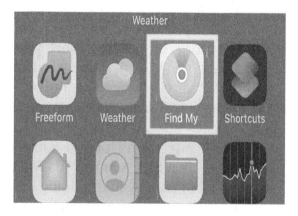

   - Provided you have Family Sharing set up and selected to share your location with your family members, you may also use Find My on their iPhone, iPad, or Mac
     - Alternatively, you may utilize Find My on a friend's phone and

the Help a Friend function to search iCloud for your phone.

2. Select the Devices menu. This tab is located in the lower part of the Find My screen.

  ▪ To view a list of your devices, slide up from the bottom of the screen if your iPhone isn't shown on the map.

  ▪ Check the map on iCloud to check whether the position of your iPhone is shown there. Click All Devices at the top of the Find Devices window and choose your iPhone from the list if you can't see it.

3. Verify that you can see the last known position of your phone.

  ▪ Pull up your device list from the bottom of the screen and press on your iPhone to view more precise location data. It will include the last known location's address and the time that information was sent.

  ▪ Select the phone from the All Devices option in iCloud. If a place is accessible, the map will enlarge to show its exact position.

  ▪ Too much time may have gone after your phone went offline if you are unable to see where your device is. It's also possible that you didn't activate every Find My function.

  ▪ Proceed to Enabling Notify When Found or Reporting your iPhone Lost if you are quite certain that Find My is activated on your phone.

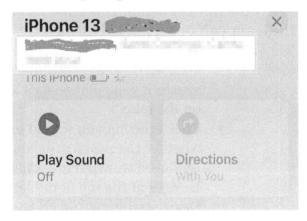

4. Use Find My to ask a friend to assist you in finding your phone.
   - On their phone, ask your buddy to launch the Find My app
   - In the bottom right corner of the screen, tap Me
   - After completing a full-screen scroll, select Help a Friend. This will launch the Find Devices page in Safari for iCloud.
   - Using the Apple ID linked to your misplaced iPhone, tap Sign In to log in. From there, you may activate Notify When Found, place your iPhone in Lost Mode, and see if the position of your phone is shown on the map.

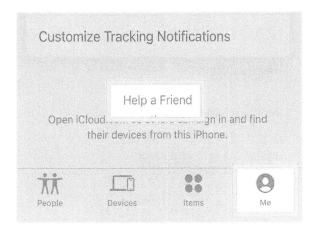

Customize Tracking Notifications

Help a Friend

Open iCloud............gn in and find
their devices from this iPhone.

People Devices Items Me

Enable Notify When found

1. Launch the Get My App app. If your iPhone reconnects to the internet and Find My can locate it, the Notify When Found setting will trigger a notice.
   - On any device, you may also use a web browser to go to https://www.icloud.com/find/ and log in using your Apple ID and password.
2. Select the Devices menu. The bottom of the app's screen is where it is.
   - On the map page, choose All Devices if you are utilizing the iCloud website.
3. From the device list, pick your iPhone.
   - Locate and choose your phone from the drop-down menu that displays when you click All Devices on the iCloud website.

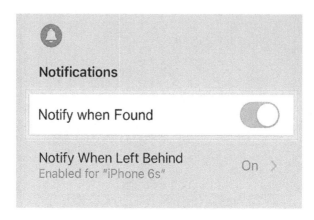

4. Turn on Notify Me When Found
   - In iCloud, choose the checkbox next to "Notify me when found" located beneath your iPhone's photo.
   - You'll receive a notification from Find My on any linked Apple devices the next time your misplaced iPhone is powered on and online.

Notifying Someone That Your iPhone Was Lost

1. Open the Find My application
   - Use the same Apple ID that you used to log into your missing iPhone when you visit https://www.icloud.com/find in a web browser if you don't have access to another Apple device
2. Click on the Devices menu. Find the Devices tab at the bottom of the Find My screen, then touch on it.
   - Click All Devices at the top of the map if you're using iCloud.
3. From the options, choose the missing iPhone.

- Select your iPhone from the All Devices dropdown option if you're using iCloud.

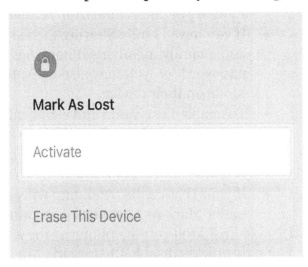

4. Under Mark, As Lost, tap Activate. This option is located towards the bottom of your device's menu.

- Select Lost Mode from the menu beneath the photo of your iPhone in iCloud

5. Pay attention to the directions on the screen.
   - Once finished, choose Activate from Find My or click Done from iCloud.
   - If you have Family Sharing turned on and a family member's iPhone has a password set, you may also activate Lost Mode on their device.
   - To enable Lost Mode and establish a pass-code for their phone if they don't already have one, you'll need to sign into iCloud with their Apple ID.
   - If your iPhone dies, Pending will appear under Mark As Lost until it reconnects
6. Disable Lost Mode on the phone or the app. You may quickly disable the missing Mode on your iPhone in a few different ways if you discover it or decide not to designate it missing.
   - If the iPhone is with you, just switch it on and unlock it by entering the pass-code. Doing so will disable Lost Mode.
   - Return to Devices in the Find My app on another device, choose your iPhone, and then select Activated or Pending under Mark As Lost. Press the Turn Off Mark As Lost, then press Turn Off again to be sure.
   - Select your iPhone from the All Devices menu in iCloud, select Lost Mode, and then select Stop Lost Mode. To be sure, click Stop Lost Mode once again.

Enable iPhone's Find My

1. Go to your iPhone's Settings App Icon Settings.
2. Press your moniker. It is the first item on the Settings menu
3. Click on Find My
4. Select "Find My iPhone." Positioned at the summit of the Find My Menu display
5. Open the Find My iPhone screen and go through all the options. You must activate every Find My function on your iPhone if it is missing, offline, or dead to have the best chance of recovering it. If none of the three options are already in the iPhone Switch On Icon On position, tap the toggle switches next to each one to turn it on.

   - Find My iPhone activates all of the standard functions of the Find My app, such as tracking your phone's location and remotely locking or wiping it in case it is misplaced.
   - Even when the phone is inactive or unplugged, Find My Network lets you view its position for a brief while.
   - When your phone's battery becomes dangerously low, communicate Last Location and ask it to communicate its location to Apple's servers.
   - To share the position of your phone with friends and family, you can also enable Share My position from the main Find My menu.

Ping your iPhone

If your Apple Watch or HomePod are linked, the easiest way to locate an iPhone is to instruct them to ping the phone on your behalf.

Find your iPhone with an Apple Watch

1. To access the Control Centre on your Apple Watch, slide up from the bottom of the screen
2. The ping button is represented by an iPhone icon with curved lines coming out of it on the left. Press it
3. At this point, if the iPhone and Apple Watch are reachable, the iPhone will "ding" at this moment to allow you to hear its whereabouts
4. Continue pinging the phone until it is located.

Find your iPhone with a HomePod

Additionally, you can use your HomePod to ping your iPhone.

1. Say, "Hey Siri, where's my iPhone?" to your HomePod
2. Hopefully, Siri will say, "I found [name's] iPhone nearby, should I make it play a sound?" if the iPhone is close enough
3. Accept and keep an ear out for your phone.

For this to function, you might need to enable Personal Requests; if so, proceed with the instructions below. You will require a device—ideally an iPad—that has the Home app installed on it. The device you are using must also have iCloud Keychain installed for the service to function.

1. On your device, launch the Home app
2. Launch the Home application
3. Press the symbol for Home
4. Press the name button
5. Activate Personal Requests on the relevant device or devices.

Launch Find My App

If you put "Find" into the search box on an iPhone, it should display in the recommendations area (same symbol as above). Drag down from the middle of the screen.

Sign in to Find My

You may click the Find My symbol on iCloud.com or open the Find My app on your Apple device. If this isn't your device, you will need to enter your Apple ID and password; this is the login you use to make purchases from the App Store and to access any other Apple services.

Sign-In Required
[YOUR LOGIN IS HERE]

Password

Sign In

Find your lost device

- You will see a list of Devices if you are using an iPhone or iPad; this list includes all of the devices that are connected to your account, including Macs, iPhones, iPads, Apple Watches, AirPods, and iPads. If you have Family Sharing enabled, the devices owned by your family members will appear below that list.
- To view all of your devices if you're using iCloud, select All Devices at the top of the window.

- On the gadget you're looking for, click or tap. As the device is being located, you could notice a spinning icon; simply wait for Find My to locate it.

Play a sound on your device

- You can use the Find My app to play a sound on your iPhone if, after finding it using the Find My app, you realize it's not too far away and you can hear it if it makes a sound.
- Simply press the Play Sound button on an iPhone
- Tap Play Sound if you're using iCloud. Before you can access the Play Sound option while using Find My on a Mac, you must click on the grey information box that is connected to the device's position on the map.

Mark your iPhone as lost

- On an iPad, Mac, or iPhone, select Activate from the Mark As Lost menu.
- Click on Lost Mode if you are accessing Find My via iCloud

Notify When Found
You will receive a notification when the location becomes available.

Activation Lock
This iPad is linked to your Apple ID so no one else can use it.

Passcode Required
Your iPad cannot be unlocked until the correct passcode has been entered.

iPad Protected
Payment cards and other services will be suspended as a safety precaution.

Leave a Message
Leave a number and message to be displayed for the person who finds this iPad.

Input your message & phone number

- You will then have the option to provide the person who finds your lost device your contact information after selecting Mark As Lost, which should assist them in getting it back to you
- Input the data, press or touch Activate.

Erase your device

It's best to wipe the iPhone if there's no chance of getting it back.

1. Select Erase This Device,
2. Click or press Continue.

You may restore the iPhone from the backup, which you should already have in iCloud if you are successful in recovering it.

As an alternative

1. Click Erase
2. Input your Apple ID password and
3. Press or click Erase again.

You may click Cancel Erase, but you'll have to enter your password again if you change your mind.

Find an iPhone belonging to a friend or family member

If you're using an iPhone 16:

1. Launch Find My
2. Press the "Me" symbol. You may need to press and drag up the Me tab to make it expand after it opens at the bottom of the screen. To view this section, drag up

3. The Help a Friend link is located at the bottom. When you select Help a Friend, iCloud.com will launch on your iPhone
4. You can choose to sign in with a different identity or as yourself. In this instance, your buddy has to log in, so please tap in. Switch up your Apple ID
5. To access their own Find My app, your buddy must now log in using their Apple ID and password.

Ask your buddy to use iCloud.com to log into their Apple ID on a Mac, PC, or other device.

CHAPTER 18
AIRTAG

Pair your iPhone with my AirTag

1. Verify iOS 17 or later
2. Launch the Find My App app
3. Click on "Add" and choose "AirTag."
4. Move the AirTag near the iPhone.
5. Give AirTag a name
6. Connect to Apple ID
7. Everything is set up. Track possessions with the Find My app.

Reset AirTag

1. Launch the iPhone app Find My
2. Find the AirTag and click on it
3. To reset, tap "Remove Item" and confirm.

Rename your AirTag

After the first setup, you may rename your AirTag.

1. Get the "Find My" app open
2. Find the AirTag and grasp its name
3. After entering the new name, click "Done."

Transfer your iPhone's AirTag to a new one

1. older iPhone
7. Choose AirTag from 'Find My' and then hit "Remove Item"
2. Configure iPhone
8. Install the most recent version of iOS.
9. Utilizing your Apple ID, log into iCloud.
3. Resetting your AirTag
   - Detach it.
   - To reset, open the rear, take out the battery, and put it back in five times.
4. Pairing:
   - Place AirTag close to the recently purchased iPhone.
   - To name and register an AirTag, follow the instructions
5. Confirmation:
   - Access 'Find My' on the latest iPhone.
   - Look for AirTag under 'Items'.

Disconnect your iPhone from my AirTag

1. Launch the Find My app
2. Choose your AirTag under Items
3. Select Remove Item and make sure

Next, the AirTag and your Apple ID will no longer be associated.

Find & access your AirTag

1. Launch the Get My App app
2. To display AirTags and trackable items, tap the Items tab.

Features of AirTags

1. Locate: Tapping on the AirTag will reveal its position on a map
2. Play Sound: To hear the AirTag beep, tap "Play Sound" if the object is close by
3. Lost Mode: When an item goes missing, turn it on. When it's located, you'll receive notifications, and the finder will have access to the shared contact details
4. Precision Finding: For comprehensive instructions to the AirTag, use this feature on iPhone 16

For optimal outcomes, don't forget to activate Bluetooth and Location Services.

Sharing AirTag with your family's

1. Select the 'Items' menu after opening the 'Find My' app on your iPhone
2. Tap the AirTag you wish to share from the list of objects
3. The 'Share This AirTag' section will include an 'Add Person' option. Click it

Share This AirTag

Add Person

Notifications

Notify When Left Behind

Lost Mode

Enabled

Rename Item

Remove Item

4. Press 'Continue' to share the chosen AirTag

Cancel

Share This AirTag

Wallet

You're the owner

Others can locate this AirTag
Everyone who shares this AirTag can
locate it in Find My

Tracking notifications will be muted
No one who shares this AirTag will get
notified when it's near them

Continue

Not Now

5. Decide which contacts to share the AirTag with. You may select a maximum of five people
6. Press the 'Send' button after choosing the contacts.

And that's it! A list of contacts with whom the selected AirTag is shared will now appear in the 'Share This AirTag' section.

Pause/End sharing AirTag

In the unlikely event that you need to deny someone access to your shared AirTag, just take these easy steps:

1. Select the shared AirTag from the 'Items' menu in the 'Find My' app
2. Tap on the name of the contact you wish to delete under the 'Share This AirTag' section.
3. The screen will display a menu at the bottom. Click "Remove."
4. Click the 'Stop Sharing' option to confirm what you just did

The owner will get a notification if the AirTag is used to track them, and they will no longer be able to follow the location of the AirTag.

CHAPTER 19

iPhone Apple Pay

Use Apple pay

If you are prepared to begin utilizing Apple Pay on your iPhone 16 and have fulfilled all the prerequisites listed in the preceding section, proceed as follows:

1. In a store that accepts Apple Pay, hold off on paying until the clerk indicates that it's time. The credit card terminal frequently features a light that lets you know when it's ready to take payment
2. Press and hold the iPhone's Side button twice.
3. Remain near the payment terminal with your iPhone
4. To utilize Face ID, confirm the purchase by glancing at your iPhone's screen
5. The iPhone screen will show a "Done" tick, and the payment terminal will advance to the following stage. In certain situations, a debit card PIN may be required

Setting your iPhone Apple Pay

Does the iPhone need an Apple Pay setup? Take these actions:

1. Launch the app Wallet
2. Press +
3. Press the Credit or Debit Card
4. Click "Continue."

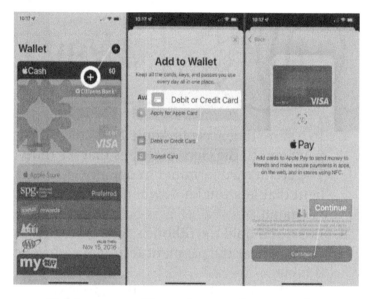

5. Hold your credit card up to the screen's viewfinder, and the Wallet app will recognize and add it. After checking the card number, click Next
6. Click Next after confirming the expiration date and adding the three-digit security code
7. Consent to the terms and conditions

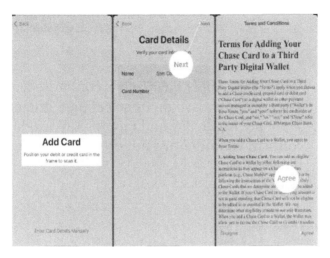

8. Choose whether to add the card to Apple Pay on Apple Watch and whether to choose the new card as your default (this will only be necessary if you have several cards registered to Apple Pay)

9. After you tap Done, the card may be used with Apple Pay in the Wallet app.

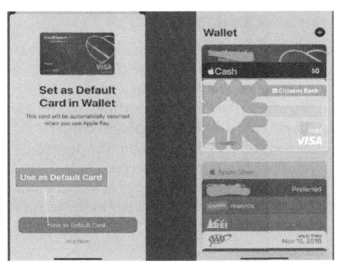

Add funds/Top Up Your Apple Pay Cash Account

1. Verify that Apple Pay Cash is configured. Toggle Apple Cash on by selecting Settings > Wallet & Apple Pay and tapping the toggle. To confirm your identity, adhere to the given procedures

2. The Wallet app has to have an Apple Pay Cash card attached to it. To use the Apple Pay Cash card, open the Wallet app and touch it.
3. To access the Cash card settings, tap the three horizontal dots in the top right corner
4. Select Add Money and input the desired amount from the bank account linked to your Cash card. You can enter a custom amount or select one from the QuickBar at the top of the dial pad. Press the "Add" button.

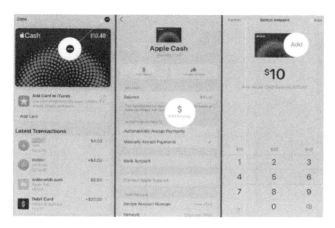

View Your Apple Pay Balance

You may check your Apple Pay Cash card balance or see whether someone has sent you money straight away by opening the Wallet app and looking at the upper right corner of the card.

1. Toggle your Apple Pay Cash card by opening the Wallet app
2. To view the card settings, tap the three horizontal dots in the top right corner
3. Your balance is shown next to the "Add Money" option.

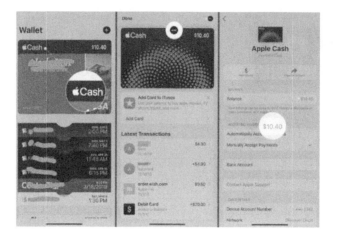

Setting your Apple Pay Cash

To initiate money transfers using Apple Pay Cash, take the following actions:

1. To access the Wallet app, tap its icon

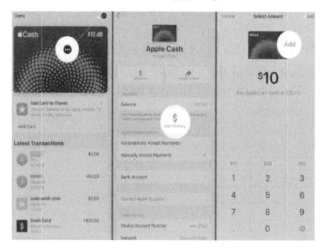

2. Press the card with Apple Pay Cash
3. Select "Set Up Now."
4. Click "Continue."

5. To accept the conditions of Apple Pay Cash, tap Agree
6. The displays below are visible. Tap Done once the blue button has stopped dimming

7. Give the Apple Pay Cash account a few moments to activate. When it's prepared, a notification displays. To hide the message, tap the X.

Make a Money Request via Apple Pay Cash

If you're owed money by someone, use Apple Pay Cash to get it back by doing the following:

1. Open Messages and start a new or join an existing discussion with that individual
2. Tap the iMessage app for Apple Pay Cash to launch it
3. Either by pressing Show Keypad or by using the + and - keys, choose the desired quantity

4. Press the Request button
5. Send the SMS after adding, if desired, a message.

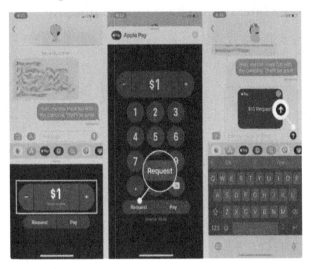

Using Apple Pay Cash to Accept Payment

1. Press the Wallet app
2. Press your Apple Pay Cash credit card
3. Press the symbol...
4. Select Manually Accept Payments from the Accepting Payments section

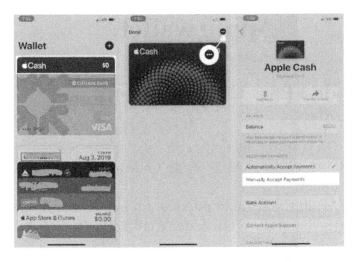

5. You must now choose Accept in the message that someone sends you whenever they send you money

Access Transaction History with Apple Pay Cash

1. Select Wallet > Apple Cash card > press the... symbol on your iPhone
2. This is a list of your most recent transactions. Tap one to see more details about it.
3. Swipe a year to view previous transactions. After that, touch a transaction to see additional details.

Apple wallet

Include a Pass Using a QR Code or Barcode

1. On your mobile, open the Wallet app
2. Select Edit Passes > Scan Code after swiping down
3. Await the scanner's activation before scanning the barcode or QR code. Your Apple Wallet now has the pass.

Utilize Wallet Pass on Apple

It's simple to access and use your Apple Wallet once you've added a pass.

Make Use of a Retail Store Pass

Retail shop loyalty cards, coupons, or incentives make up the majority of wallet passes. It's easy to use a card in a physical store once you've added these cards to your Wallet.

1. Launch the app Wallet
2. Scroll through your wallet to find the pass you want to use
3. To examine the pass's information, including the barcode or QR code, tap it

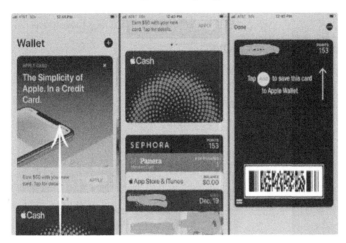

4. The cashier scans the code from your mobile when you're in a store

Utilize a boarding pass

1. Open your Apple Wallet and find your boarding pass
2. Before you go through security and at the gate to board your aircraft, scan your mobile boarding pass
3. To see the boarding passes you have available, swipe left and right. Your boarding cards are kept together in the Wallet in case your vacation consists of several legs or flights.

Delete pass from Your Wallet

1. Locate the pass you wish to delete by opening the Wallet app
2. In the upper-right corner of the screen, press the pass and then hit More (three dots)
3. To remove it from your wallet, select Remove Pass > Remove.

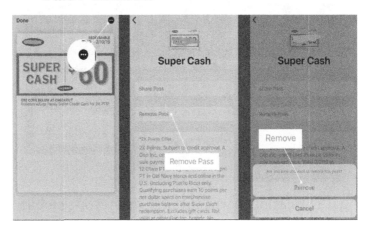

Adding Credit Card to Apple Wallet

1. Click Add (+ sign) in the upper-right corner of the Wallet app after opening it
2. Select Debit or Credit Card
3. Select "Continue."
4. Scan your card or manually input the credit card information. To confirm your card details, tap Next.
5. Tap Next after entering your security code
6. To accept the terms and conditions, tap Agree. Your card is verified by Wallet

7. Select a verification technique, then press Next. **NOTE: You can instead select Finish Verification Later**

8. Your wallet now has your card. Select either Use as Default Card or Not Now.

9. **NOTE: Another option is to open the iPhone Settings, select Wallet & Apple Pay, and then select Add Card.**

How to Include a Credit Card in Apple Wallet

1. Either select Settings > Wallet & Apple Pay or tap the Wallet app

2. Tap the + in the Wallet app or select Add Card in Settings

3. You have two options: either take a photo of your card with your camera to have it automatically fill in the details, or manually input the information according to the onscreen instructions

4. After you enter your card information, Apple may need some time to confirm the details with your bank before your card appears in the Wallet app and you can use Apple Pay with it

5. Carry out this procedure for every credit or debit card that you wish to include in your wallet. Regardless of how many cards you have in your Wallet, you may choose which card to use when making payments with Apple Pay.

How to Use iCloud to Remove a Card from Apple Pay

Access iCloud to Track Down Your Lost Phone

1. Open a web browser on any device—desktop, laptop, iPhone, or other mobile device—and navigate to iCloud.com.
2. Sign in with the credentials from your iCloud account—which, depending on how you set up iCloud, are probably the same as your Apple ID username and password
3. Select iCloud Settings by clicking on the Settings button or by clicking on your name in the upper right corner of the iCloud.com page after logging in
4. Unlike your Apple ID or iCloud account, your Apple Pay information is linked to each device it is set up on. That's why you need to go to the My Devices area and locate the stolen phone. By placing an Apple Pay symbol underneath each device, Apple makes it simple to identify which ones have Apple Pay set up
5. To open it in a new window, click the stolen iPhone that has the card you wish to erase
6. Below the Apple iPhone, the cards you have listed on your iPhone are shown in the image. Select delete Everything
7. To finish deleting your bank information, choose Remove on the confirmation box that appears.

CHAPTER 20

Camera Guide

Take a picture

1. Navigate to your device's camera
2. Click on the camera icon
3. Focus your camera on the subject you would like to capture
4. Press the red circular icon in the middle

Record a video with your device

1. Navigate to your device's camera
2. Click the camera icon
3. Focus your camera on the subject you would like to record
4. Press down the circular red icon in the middle
5. Once you are done recording remove your finger from the pressed-down circular red icon
6. Your video will automatically saved to your video folder, album, or gallery

Recording & cropping a video.

Few people are aware that you may crop films to make them square or rectangular using the video editing features on your iPhone.

1. Just click on the Camera Roll
2. Pick the video
3. Select "Edit."
4. Click the far right crop tool

5. To adjust the video's cropping, drag the white lines at the top and bottom with your index finger.

Note that all pictures taken or videos recorded will be automatically saved to the photo app

Hide Pictures on your device

some pictures are meant for your privacy and you wouldn't like that relative or friends to have access to them, here is a tip on how to hide them

1. Press the picture menu on your device
2. Locate the picture you wish to conceal and press the share icon located in the lower left corner
3. Move your cursor down until the "hide" option appears
4. Click "Hide photo"
5. Click the albums menu located at the bottom of your camera roll to view your hidden photographs
6. Under Utilities, scroll down until you locate the Hidden menu
7. All of the concealed pictures in your "hidden album" will be displayed to you.

Live Pictures

Live Photos are turned on by default. Moreover, disabling it through the camera app, which is the most obvious method, is not a long-term solution. Unless you take further action, you'll discover that the function is back on soon.

Temporarily toggle off Live Pictures

1. Open the Camera app and search for the button for Live Photos
2. Give the bullseye a tap.

Deactivate Live Pictures

Follow these instructions to fully disable Live Photos. You may switch on Live Photos again by repeating these steps later and reversing the modifications.

1. Choose Settings
2. Press the Camera button
3. Toggle the button next to Live Photos by clicking Preserve Settings.

Adjusting your live pictures

You may alter the primary display frame and apply a variety of modifications and effects to each Live Photo.

1. From the Albums pane in the Photo app, open a Live Photo and select Edit.
2. Tap the bullseye icon to switch the frame that serves as the still image

3. Use your finger to move the bottom slider, then let go when you've found the desired frame
4. Press the icon for "Make Key Photo."

Converting a live picture into a static picture

To turn a live photo into a static image, follow these steps:

1. Select Edit after opening your Live Photo
2. Make any necessary changes and cropping
3. To choose the frame you wish to utilize, tap the bullseye symbol
4. Tap the yellow Live tag* at the top. A strikethrough bullseye icon will appear, and the tag will turn white. Click "Done."

Your original Live Photo is still saved in the Camera Roll, but your altered version of the Live Photo is now a standard image.

Screenshot with your device

To capture a screenshot,

- Just press and hold the Power and Volume up keys at the same time.
- On the lower left portion of the screen, a little version of the screenshot will show up. If you want to make any changes, just tap the picture; if not,
- It will save to your Photos app in a matter of seconds.

Screen Record with your iPhone 16

1. Open Settings and choose Control Centre
2. Select "Customize Controls" from the menu and then "Screen Recording"
3. Go to your home screen after exiting your settings. Choose the little white circle inside the square symbol by swiping up the Control Centre. This is the symbol for screen recording.
4. Your iPhone activities will be captured once the recorder counts down from three.
5. To end the recording, touch the red recording timer located at the top of your screen. Your recording is located on your camera roll, where you may edit it using the same tools as a regular video, such as cutting the beginning and ending. Alternatively, you may use the free iMovie app that comes with your iPhone to edit it.

Portrait Mode

How to use your iPhone to take portrait photos

Adding depth to the backdrop of your images will make them appear more professional. You may change the aperture of the lens to add or remove depth by taking pictures in Portrait Mode.

1. Launch the Camera app
2. Change the "Photo" to "Portrait" setting
3. Press and hold the aperture feature, indicated by the little "f" in the upper right corner
4. To alter the depth, slide to the left or right. Your shot will have greater depth if you slide to the left, and less depth if you go to the right
5. Press the shutter button to take a picture after you are satisfied with the depth of field. You may always press the "Edit" option to change the depth of your Portrait Mode photo if you don't achieve the ideal snap.

Even though Portrait Mode saves you a lot of effort, there are a few things to keep in mind while attempting to capture that incredible moment!

- If you are not at least two meters away from the subject, Portrait Mode will not be enabled.
- Press and hold the item or person you wish to concentrate on with your finger on the camera if your camera is having trouble focusing.
- If you adjust the depth of field too much, the backdrop will become so blurry that it becomes completely invisible. A picturesque subject, like

as a mountain or the ocean, calls for a shallow depth of field.

Burst mode

How to use your iPhone's burst mode for photography

In burst mode, you may snap many pictures by pressing and holding down the white shutter button. It is sometimes referred to as burst shot, high-speed mode, or sports mode. Sports, animals in motion, and fast-moving subjects make for the finest subjects for burst mode photography.

Here is how to do it

1. Launch the Camera app
2. Use your finger to depress the white shutter button. This will capture several pictures simultaneously, or a "burst" of pictures
3. After you're done, you should select the best one. Press "Select."
4. Navigate through the collection of pictures and select your favorite. After selecting "Done," choose "Keep Only One Favourite" or "Keep Everything."

Recording a slow-mo video

Record slow-motion videos via your device

Seize those magnificent, quick-moving moments that are best experienced in slow motion.

1. Launch the Camera app
2. To begin recording, slide from "Photo" to "Slo-Mo" and press the red shutter button
3. After you've completed recording, press the shutter button one more.

Editing your SLO motion video timing

It's easy to transfer the "slow motion" portion of a slo-mo video to a different location on the recording.

1. Locate a slow-motion movie in your Camera Roll that you want to modify
2. Select "Edit."
3. Use your finger to slide the white line that appears beneath the video. The white line indicates the portion of your video that is and is not in slow motion. Select the portion of your video that you wish to slow down or speed up
4. Select "Done."

Spatial videos

Use your device to record spatial video

Enable spatial video

Turn on your device's spatial video

1. You cannot just search for "spatial" in Settings by dragging down the search bar. This produces a large, blank, white screen
2. Navigate down the Settings app until the Camera app appears
3. At this point, select the Formats menu item:
4. Turn on Spatial Video for Apple Vision Pro by swiping down until you see it.

Alternatively

Enable spatial video via settings

- Toggle the Spatial Video for Apple Vision Pro option to on in the Camera settings of the main Settings app. Next,
- Choose Formats.

Display/brightness
Adjust the display's brightness on your iPhone

Depending on your preferences while taking a picture, you may adjust the brightness of your screen.

1. Open the Settings app.
2. Select "Display & Brightness"
3. To adjust the brightness and contrast of your display, slide the slider to the right or left.

With its unique True Tone ambient light sensor, your iPhone can also detect ambient light conditions to determine the optimal screen brightness. Thus, if you want your screen brightness to decide for you, do the following:

1. Select Settings
2. Select Brightness & Display
3. Turn on the True Tone.

Dark mode
Use the Dark Mode feature

1. Select Settings
2. Select "Brightness and Display."
3. Select "Dark Mode."
4. Turn "Automatic" on so that Dark Mode activates on its own when the sun sets

By choosing the dark interface, you may also permanently set Dark Mode if you like the way it looks.

Wallpaper

Customize/Modify the wallpaper on your iPhone

You may choose one of the wallpaper selections that came with your iPhone, or you can use a picture that you took.

1. Launch the Photos app
2. Choose the image you want to use as your wallpaper
3. Tap the "Share" button located in the lower-left corner of the screen
4. Select "Use as Wallpaper" by scrolling
5. Toggle to modify, then press "Set."

Alternatively, you might use the Settings app to accomplish it.

1. Select Settings
2. Launch the wallpaper
3. Select "Select a New Wallpaper."
4. Select a wallpaper from the collection of ready-made designs or a picture from your camera roll
5. Select which screen the wallpaper is for by tapping "Set" after that. The lock screen, your home screen, or both

Book index

T

U

V

W

Made in the USA
Las Vegas, NV
08 November 2024

11385003R00118